This Breathing Book Belongs To:

_____

_____

Rainbow Breathing Book

· ★ · ★ · ★ · ★ · ★ · ★ · ★ · ★ · ★ · ★ · ★ · ★ · ★ · ★ · ★ · ★ · ★ ·

Hey hey!

This breathing book is designed to guide you in focusing on your breathe through a more engaging and interactive way.

You are going to love exploring the six fun breathing exercises that can help you calm down. Use them when you are experiencing a big emotion, feeling super excited, a bit wiggly, or when you just want to practice the breathing exercise.

Enjoy keeping calm and remember, you've totally got this!

Happy Breathing,
Prima from LittleYellowStar

· ★ · ★ · ★ · ★ · ★ · ★ · ★ · ★ · ★ · ★ · ★ · ★ · ★ · ★ · ★ · ★ · ★ ·

LittleYellowStar
TEACH & CREATE

Check out more books from LittleYellowStar Publishing here:

Table of Contents

Rainbow Breathing

Spiral Breathing

Triangle Breathing

Box Breathing

Lazy 8 Breathing

Star Breathing

How To Use This Book

There are multiple ways to use this book, depending on what resonates best with your child. The breathing techniques are designed to be interactive, making it easy to practice deep breathing in different ways.

Finger Tracing:

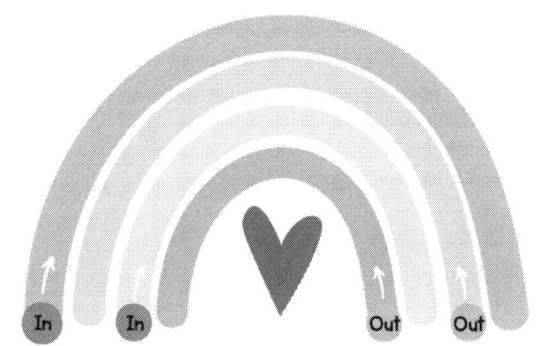

- The first two pages of every breathing exercise are dedicated to finger tracing. This is a great tactile way to practice the breathing technique.
- Encourage your child to trace each breath in and breath out for about 4 seconds. If that's a bit challenging at first, start with 1-2 seconds and gradually increase to 4.

Coloring or Using a Drawing Tool:

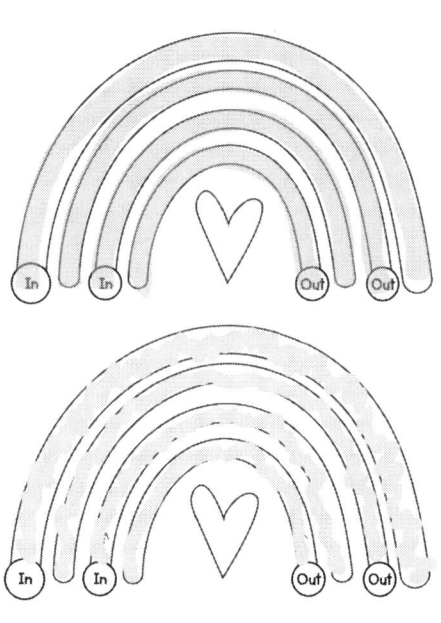

- Let your child use a crayon, colored pencil, or marker to trace or color while practicing the breathing technique.
- Warning - Markers may bleed through the pages, especially when tracing back and ford. Crayons and colored pencils are a better tool to use with this book.
- The full size breathing technique is best for tracing with a drawing tool.
- The smaller size are great for both tracing and coloring.
- Help your child work up to 4 seconds for every breath in, hold, and breath out. Starting small, such as with 2 seconds, is a great way to build confidence and skill.

Ways To Incorporate Breathing Techniques In Your Child's Daily Routine

When we think of using Calm-Down tools, we often ONLY turn to them during a child's stress or big emotional response. But actually, that's not always the best time to introduce something new, even breathing techniques.

Why? Because they are in the middle of a Fight-or-Flight response, so they are not receptive to new information. That's exactly why it's crucial to teach and practice breathing techniques with your child well in advance. Incorporating these practice into your child's daily routine makes them even more effective and easier for both of you. By practicing ahead of time, when a big emotion arises, your child will be familiar with it and can use the breathing technique of choice to calm down!

Below are 5 different ideas to incorporate breathing techniques into your child's daily routine:

⭐ **Morning Routine:**
> Start the day with a simple breathing exercise. It can set a calm tone for the day ahead. Even just a few deep breaths together can make a big difference.

⭐ **Bedtime Ritual:**
> Use breathing techniques as part of the bedtime routine. It helps children relax and wind down, making it easier to fall asleep.

⭐ **Before or After School:**
> Breathing exercises can be a great transition tool. They can help your child switch gears from home to school mode and vice versa.

⭐ **During Long Car Rides:**
> Use this time to practice breathing techniques together. It's a great way to turn potentially boring or stressful situations into moments of calm.

⭐ **Before or After Homework/Study Sessions:**
> Breathing exercises can be a great transition tool. They can help your child switch gears from home to school mode and vice versa.

Rainbow Breathing

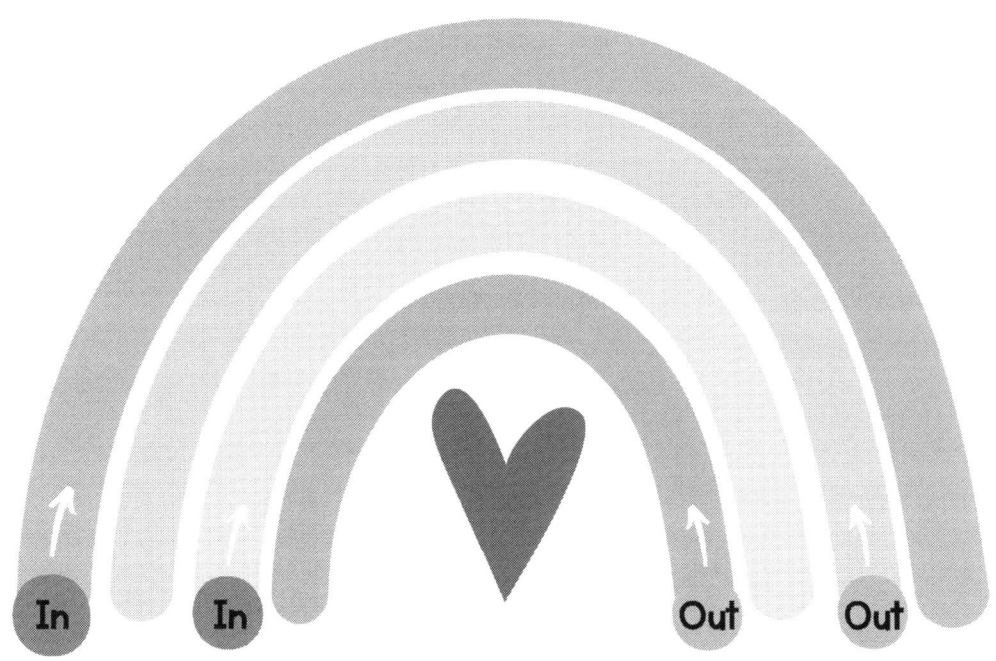

Rainbow Breathing

Directions:

Use your finger to trace the outer layer of the rainbow and breathe in. Then trace your finger on the inner layer of the rainbow and breathe out. Continue doing this for at least 5 times or until you feel calmer.

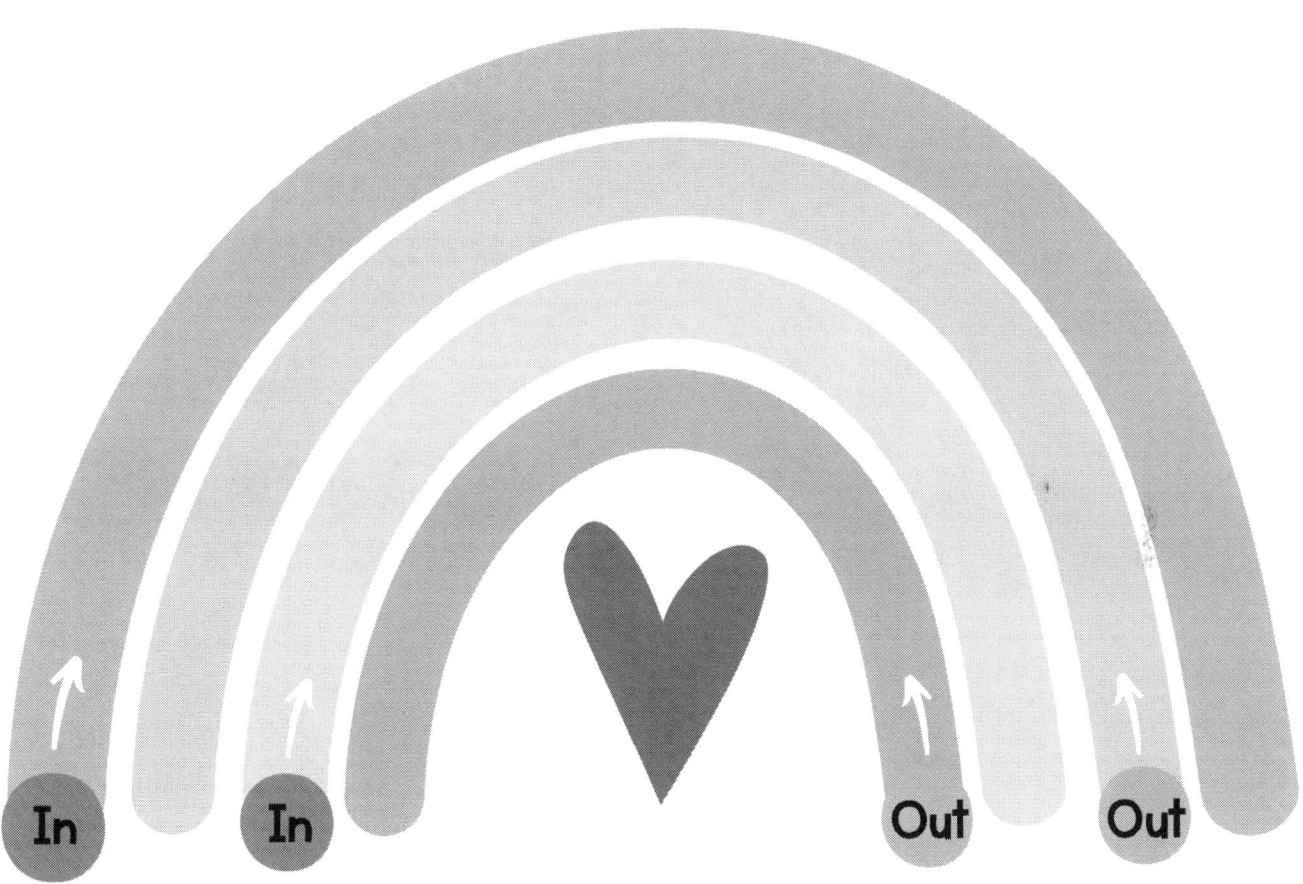

4

"Somewhere over the rainbow, skies are blue, and the dreams that you dare to dream really do come true."

- Judy Garland
"Over the Rainbow"

Rainbow Breathing

Directions:

With any drawing tool, trace the outer layer of the rainbow while breathing in. Then trace the inner layer of the rainbow while breathing out. Continue doing this at least 5 times or until you feel calmer.

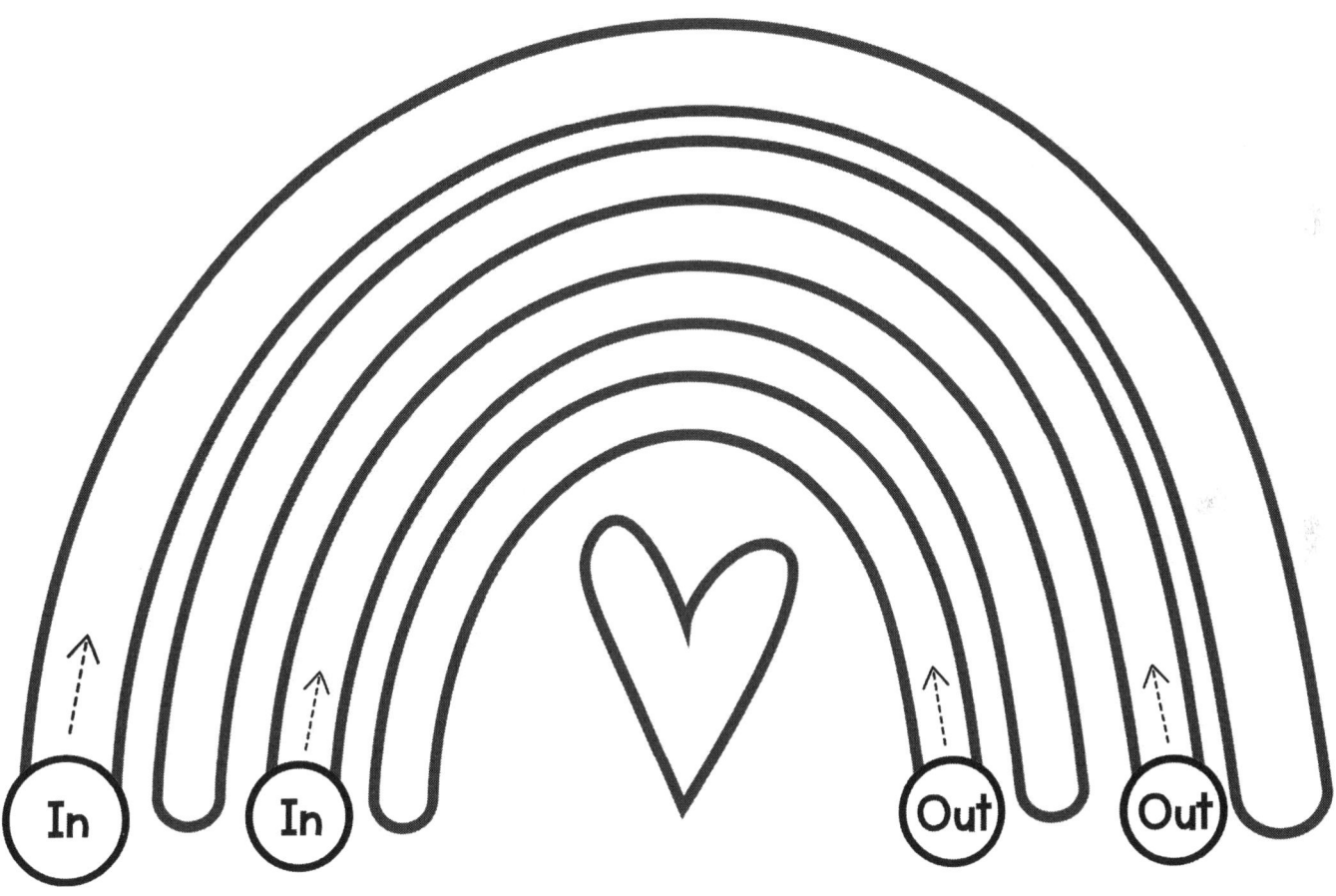

6

Rainbow Breathing

Directions:

With any drawing tool, trace the outer layer of the rainbow while breathing in. Then trace the inner layer of the rainbow while breathing out. Continue doing this at least 5 times or until you feel calmer.

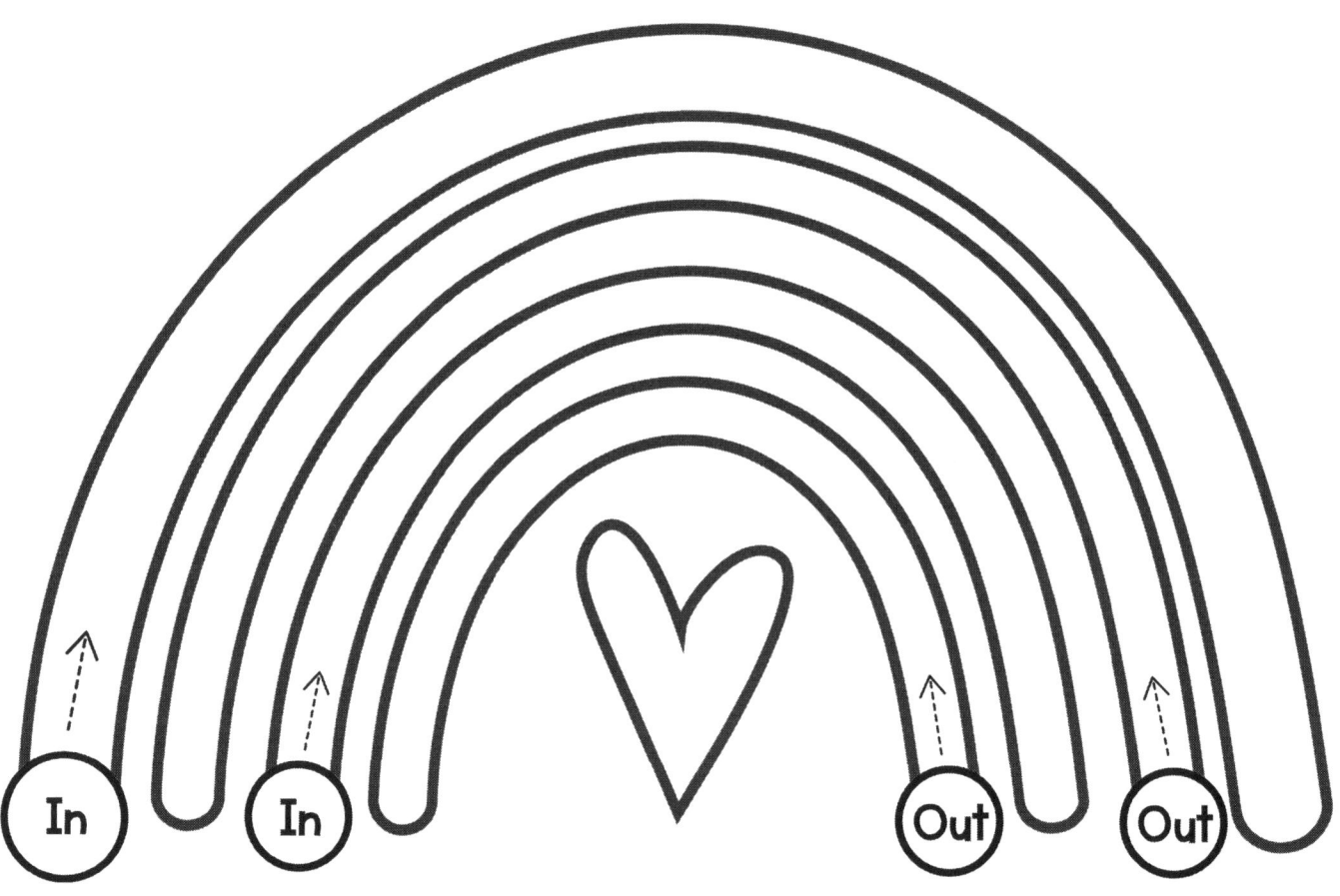

Rainbow Breathing

Directions:

With any drawing tool, trace the outer layer of the rainbow while breathing in. Then trace the inner layer of the rainbow while breathing out. Continue doing this at least 5 times or until you feel calmer.

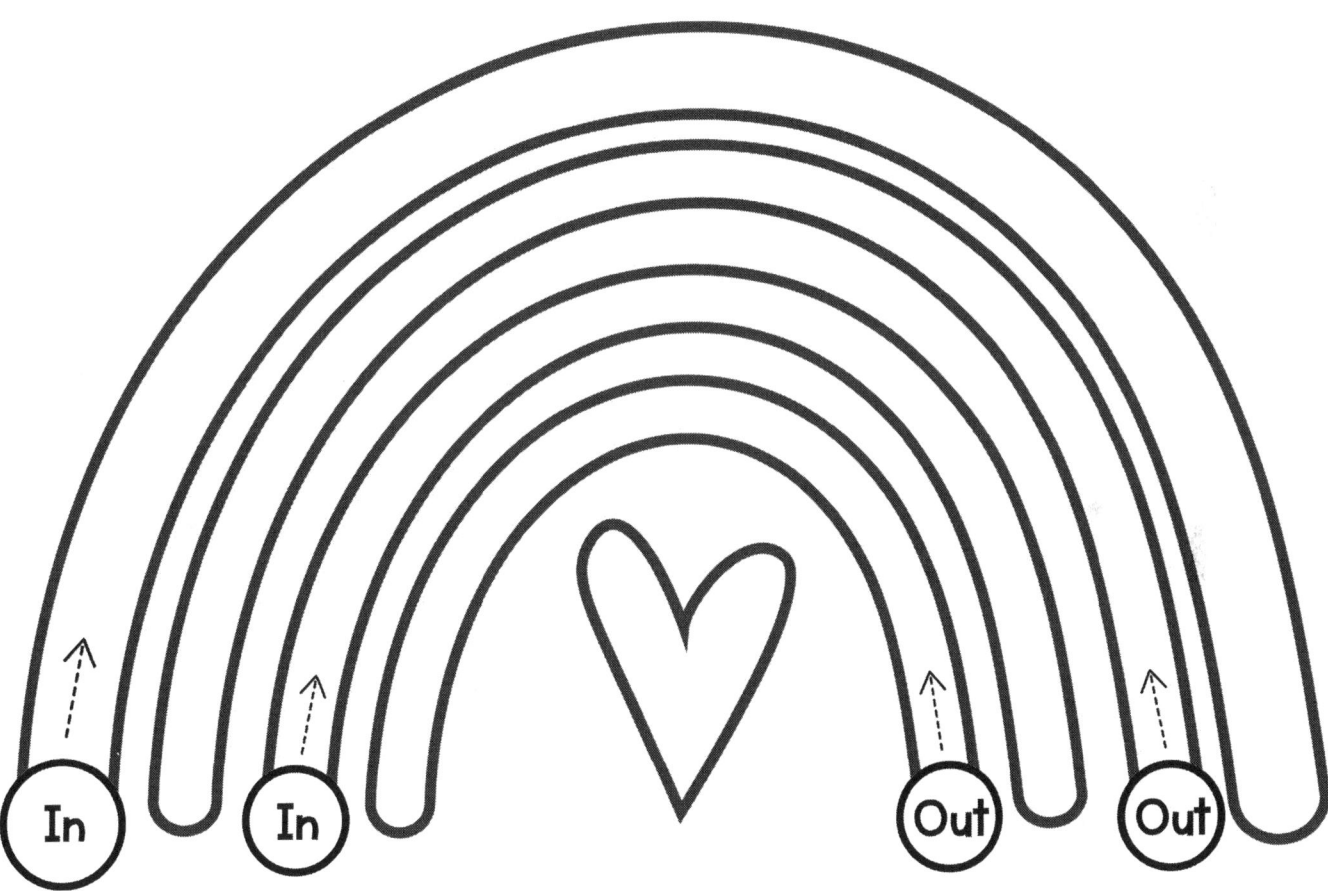

8

Rainbow Breathing

<u>Directions:</u>

With any drawing tool, trace the outer layer of the rainbow while breathing in. Then trace the inner layer of the rainbow while breathing out. Continue doing this until you feel calmer.

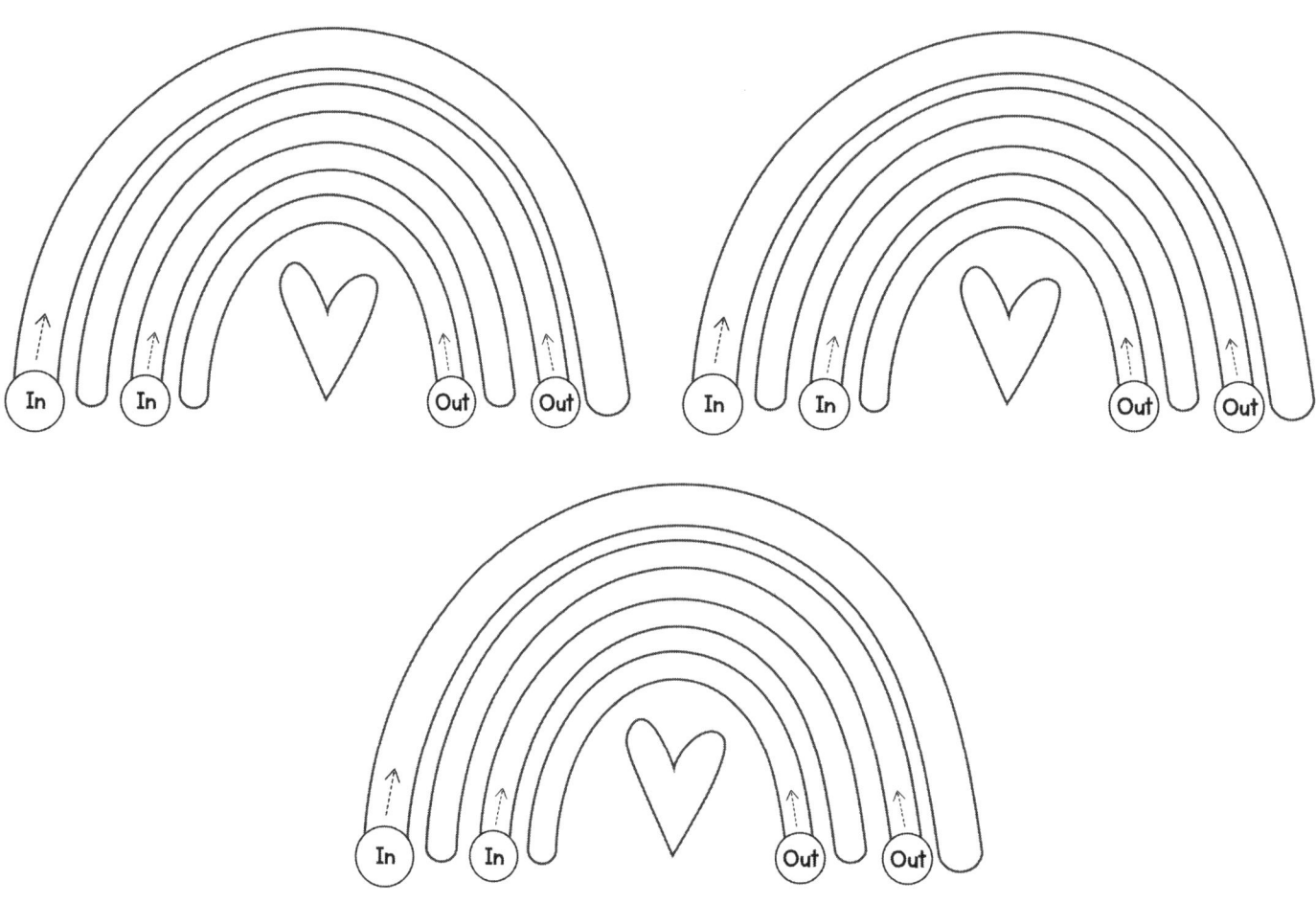

9

Rainbow Breathing

Directions:

With any drawing tool, trace the outer layer of the rainbow while breathing in. Then trace the inner layer of the rainbow while breathing out. Continue doing this until you feel calmer.

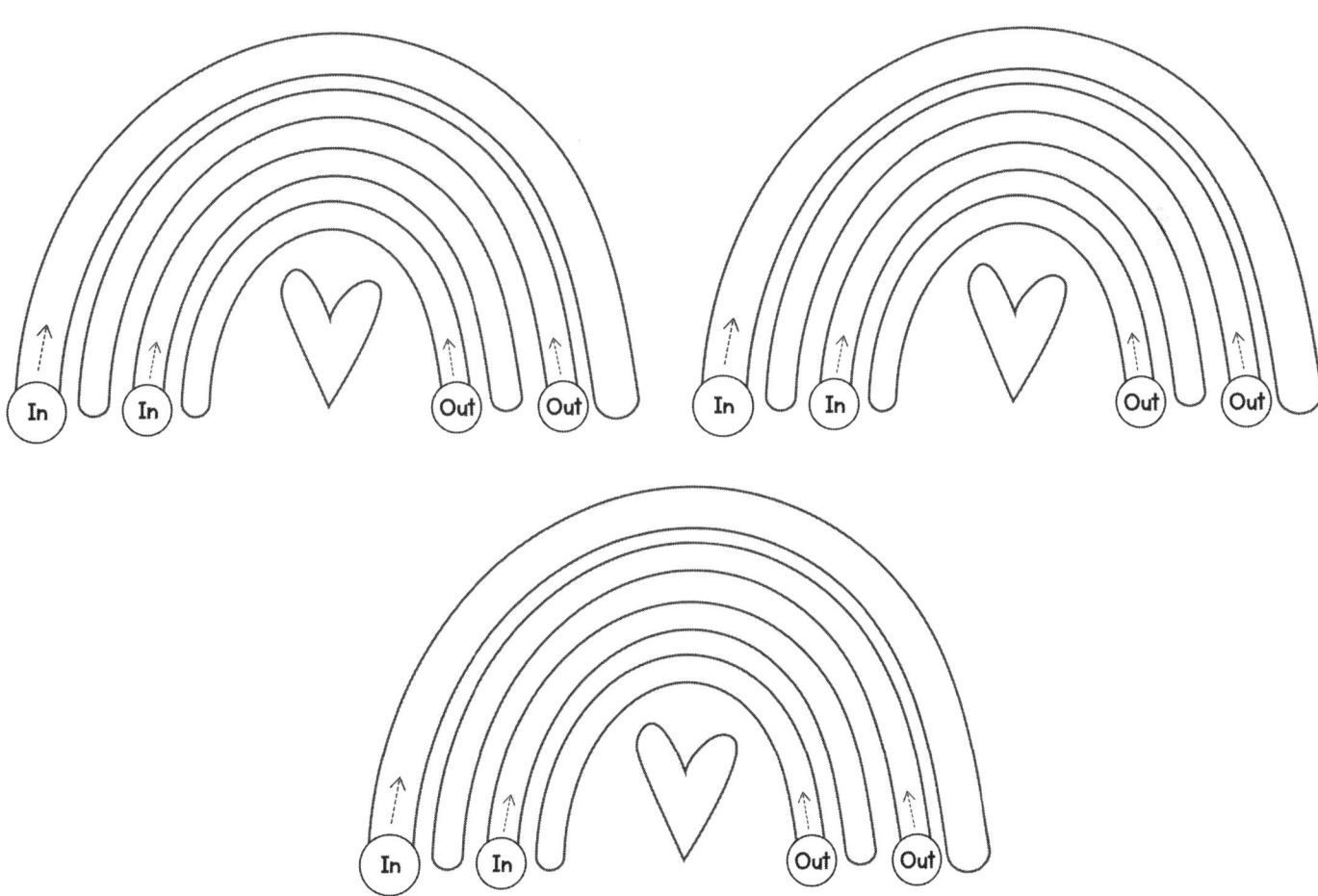

10

Rainbow Breathing

Directions:

With any drawing tool, trace the outer layer of the rainbow while breathing in. Then trace the inner layer of the rainbow while breathing out. Continue doing this until you feel calmer.

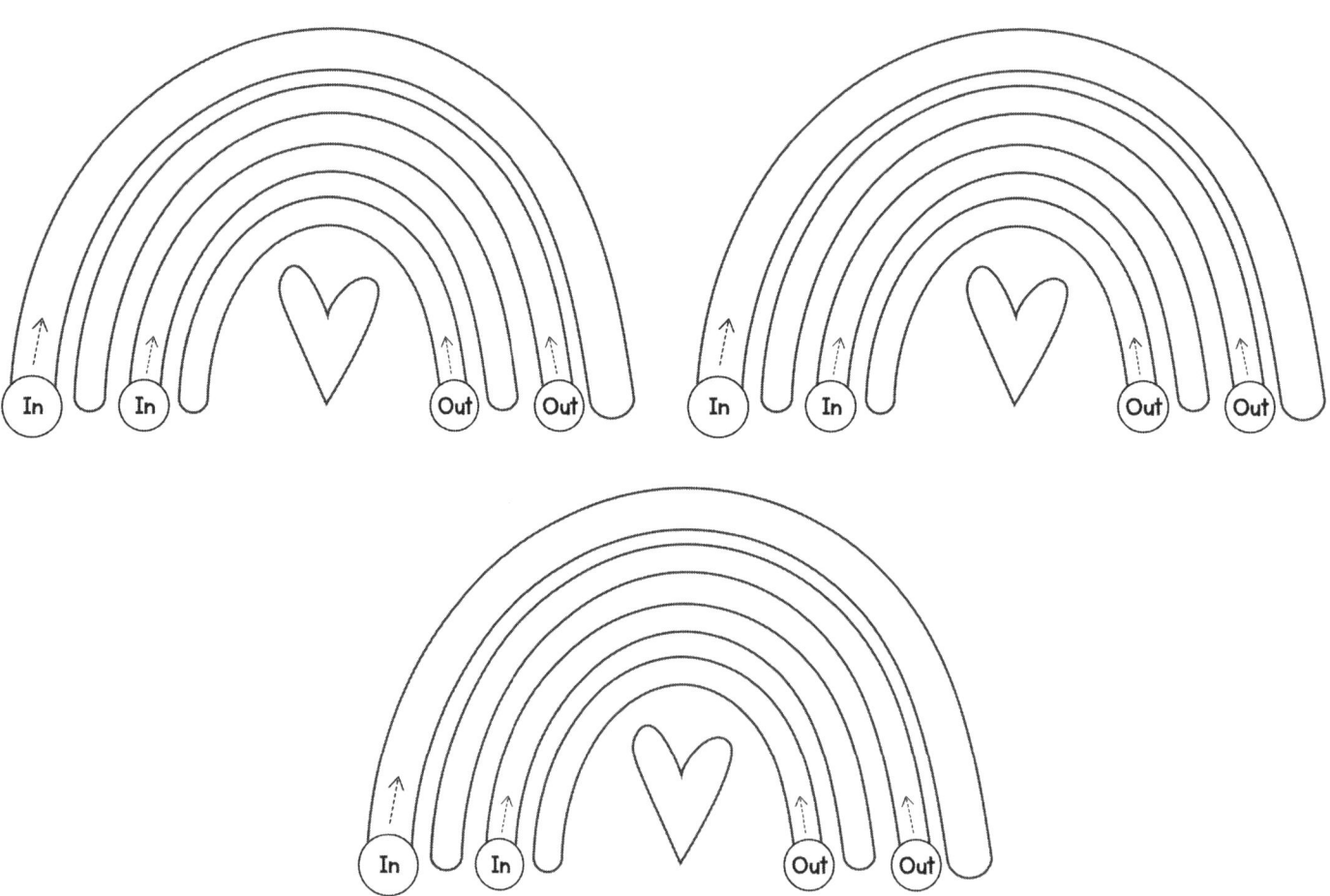

Rainbow Breathing

Directions:

With any drawing tool, trace the outer layer of the rainbow while breathing in. Then trace the inner layer of the rainbow while breathing out. Continue doing this until you feel calmer.

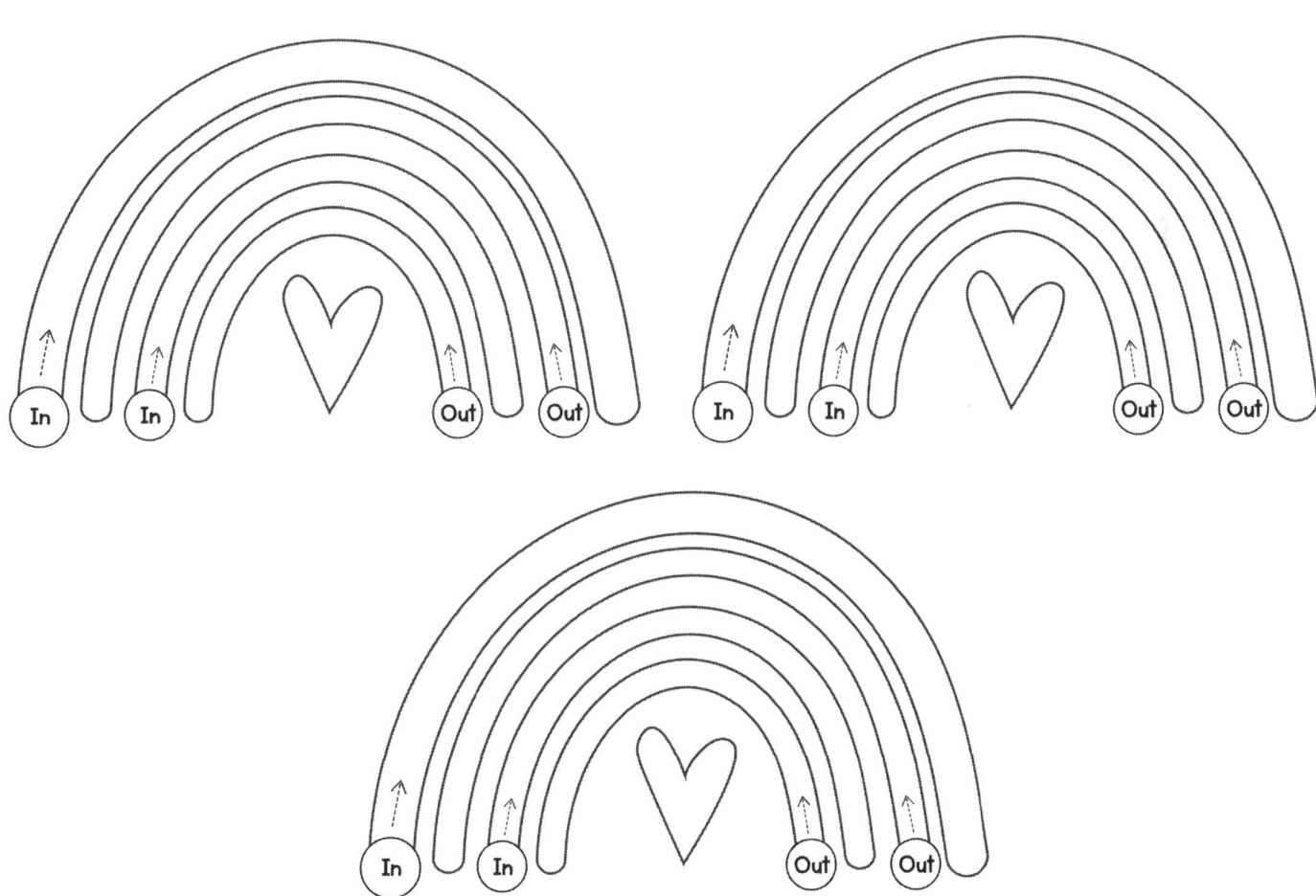

Rainbow Breathing

Directions:

With any drawing tool, trace the outer layer of the rainbow while breathing in. Then trace the inner layer of the rainbow while breathing out. Continue doing this until you feel calmer.

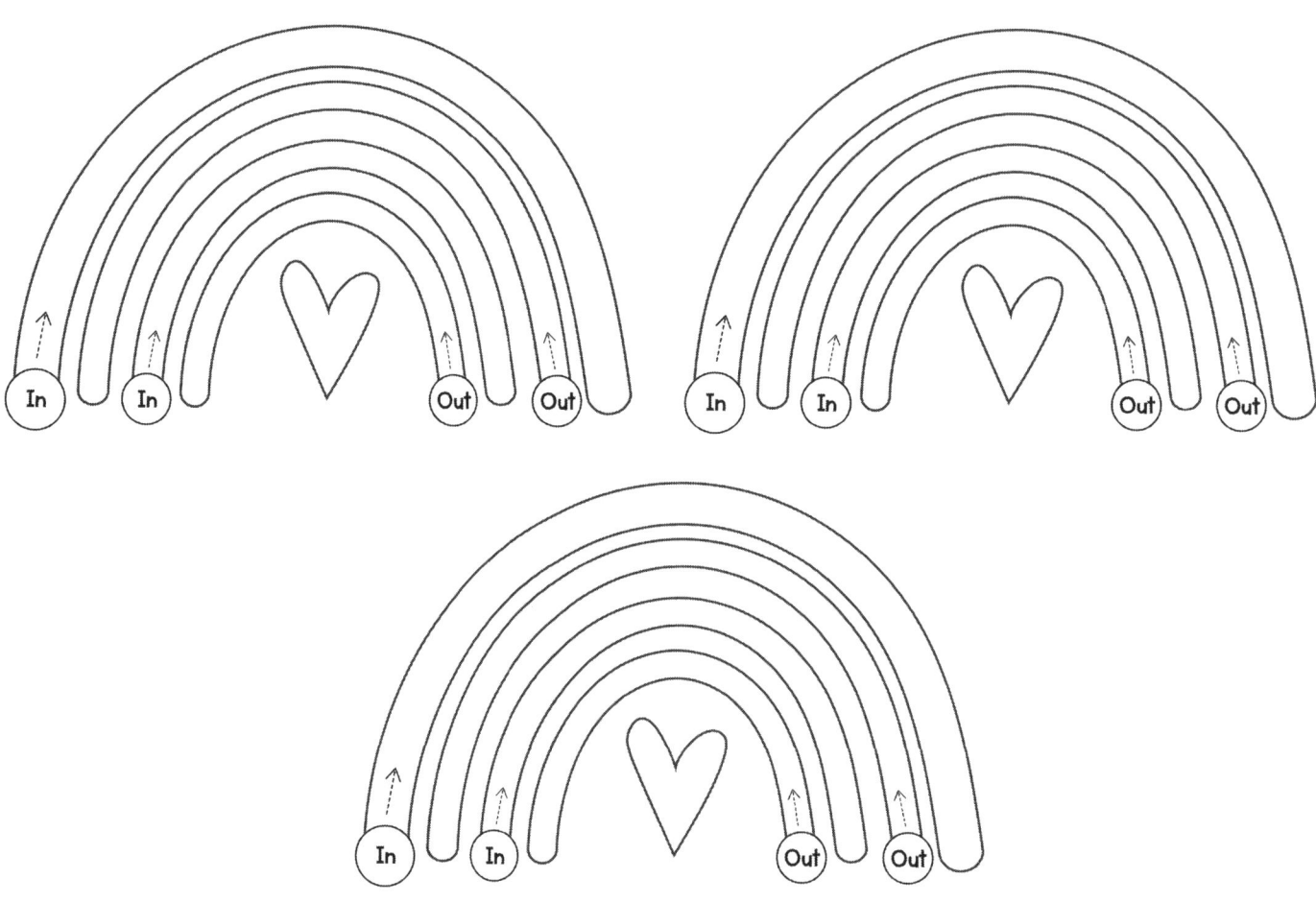

Rainbow Breathing

Directions:

With any drawing tool, trace the outer layer of the rainbow while breathing in. Then trace the inner layer of the rainbow while breathing out. Continue doing this until you feel calmer.

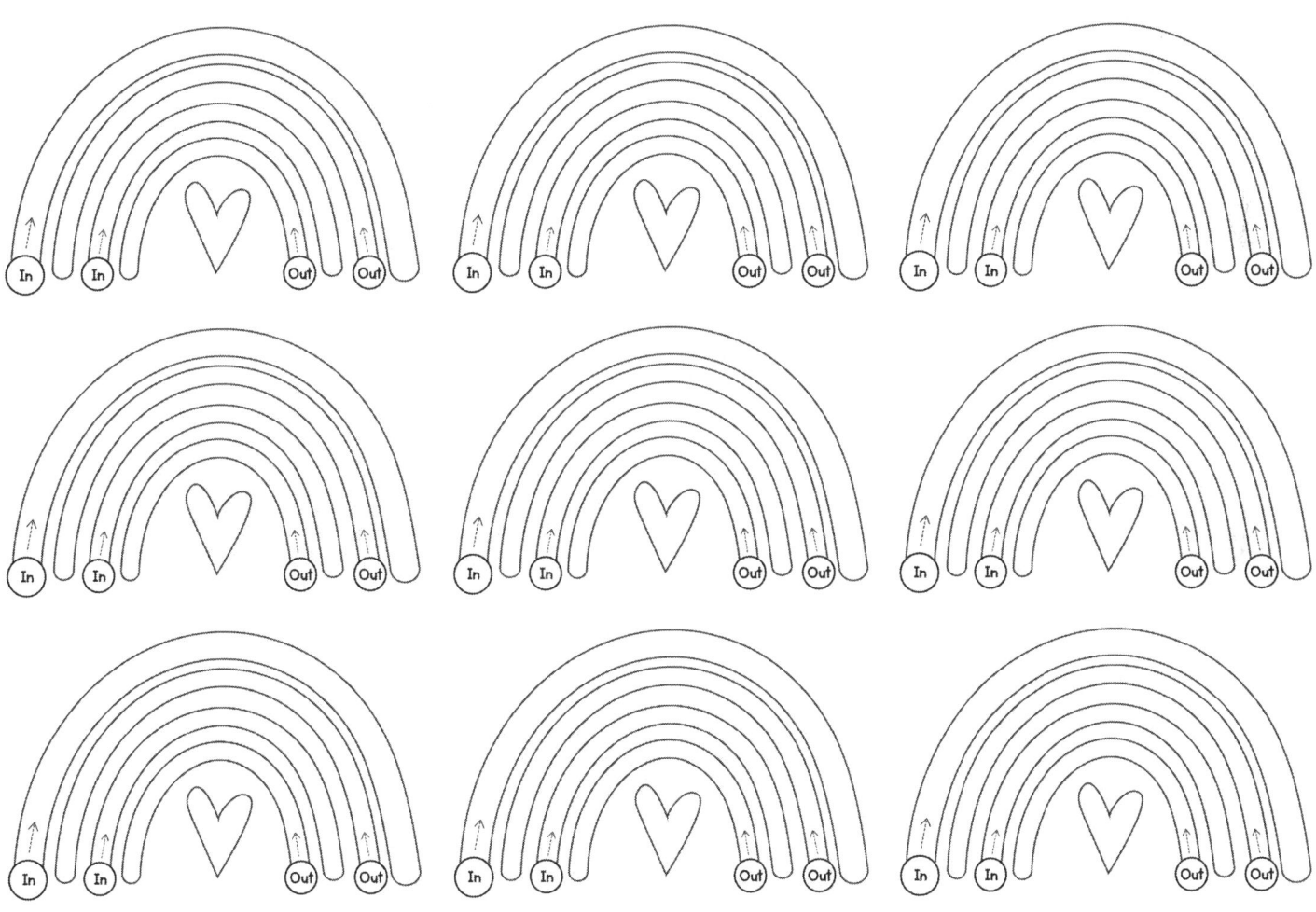

Rainbow Breathing

Directions:

With any drawing tool, trace the outer layer of the rainbow while breathing in. Then trace the inner layer of the rainbow while breathing out. Continue doing this until you feel calmer.

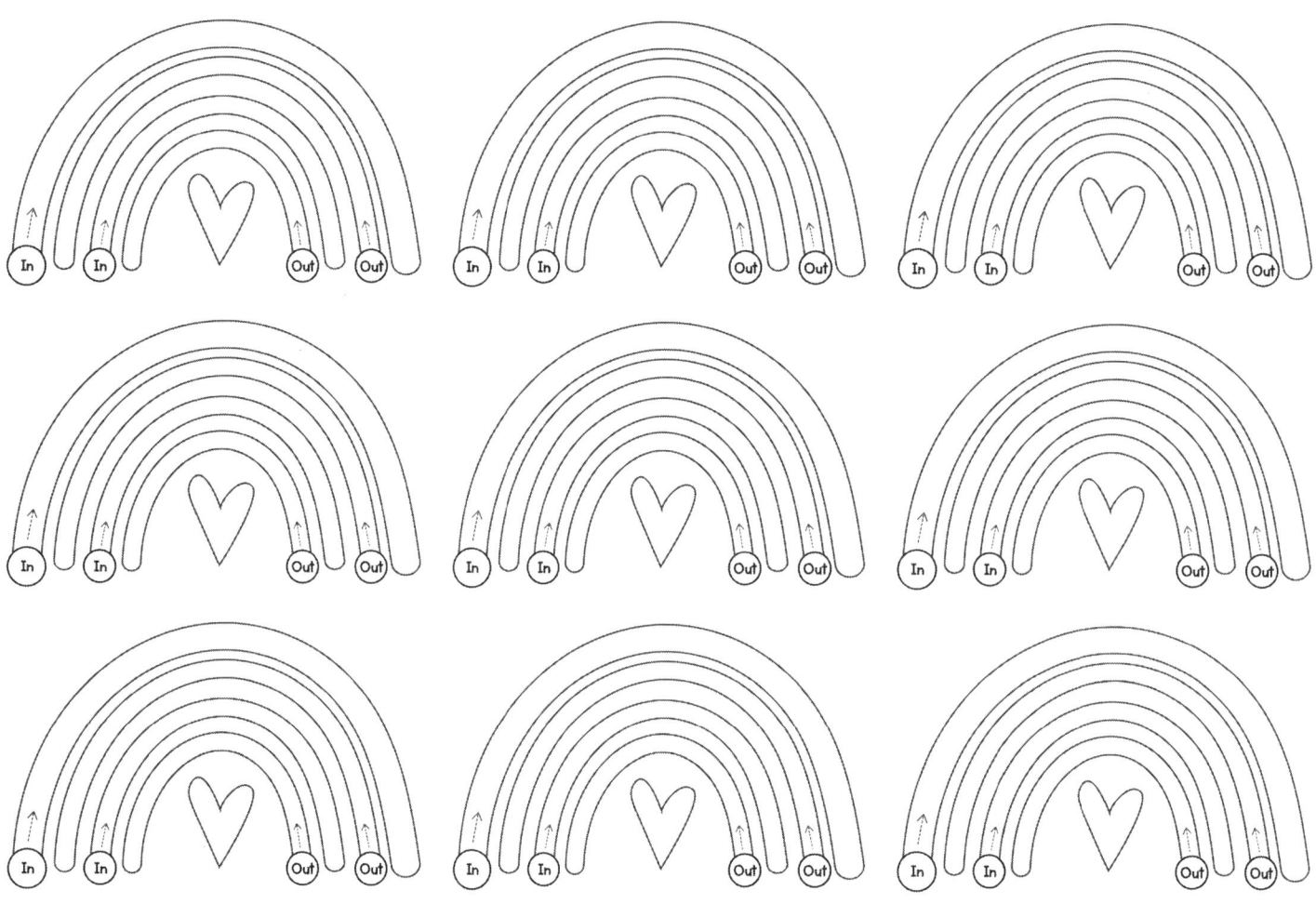

Rainbow Breathing

Directions:

With any drawing tool, trace the outer layer of the rainbow while breathing in. Then trace the inner layer of the rainbow while breathing out. Continue doing this until you feel calmer.

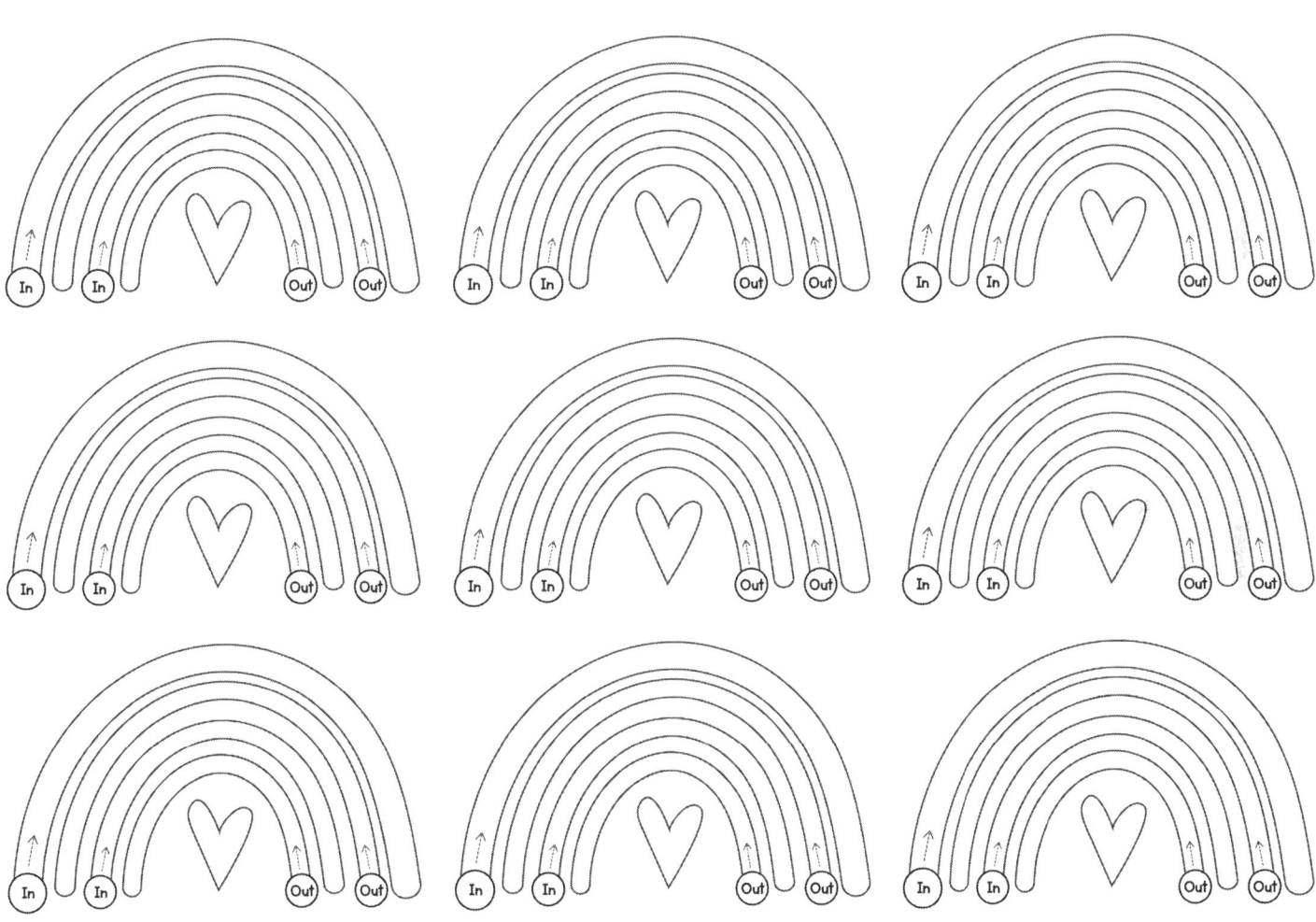

16

Rainbow Breathing

Directions:

With any drawing tool, trace the outer layer of the rainbow while breathing in. Then trace the inner layer of the rainbow while breathing out. Continue doing this until you feel calmer.

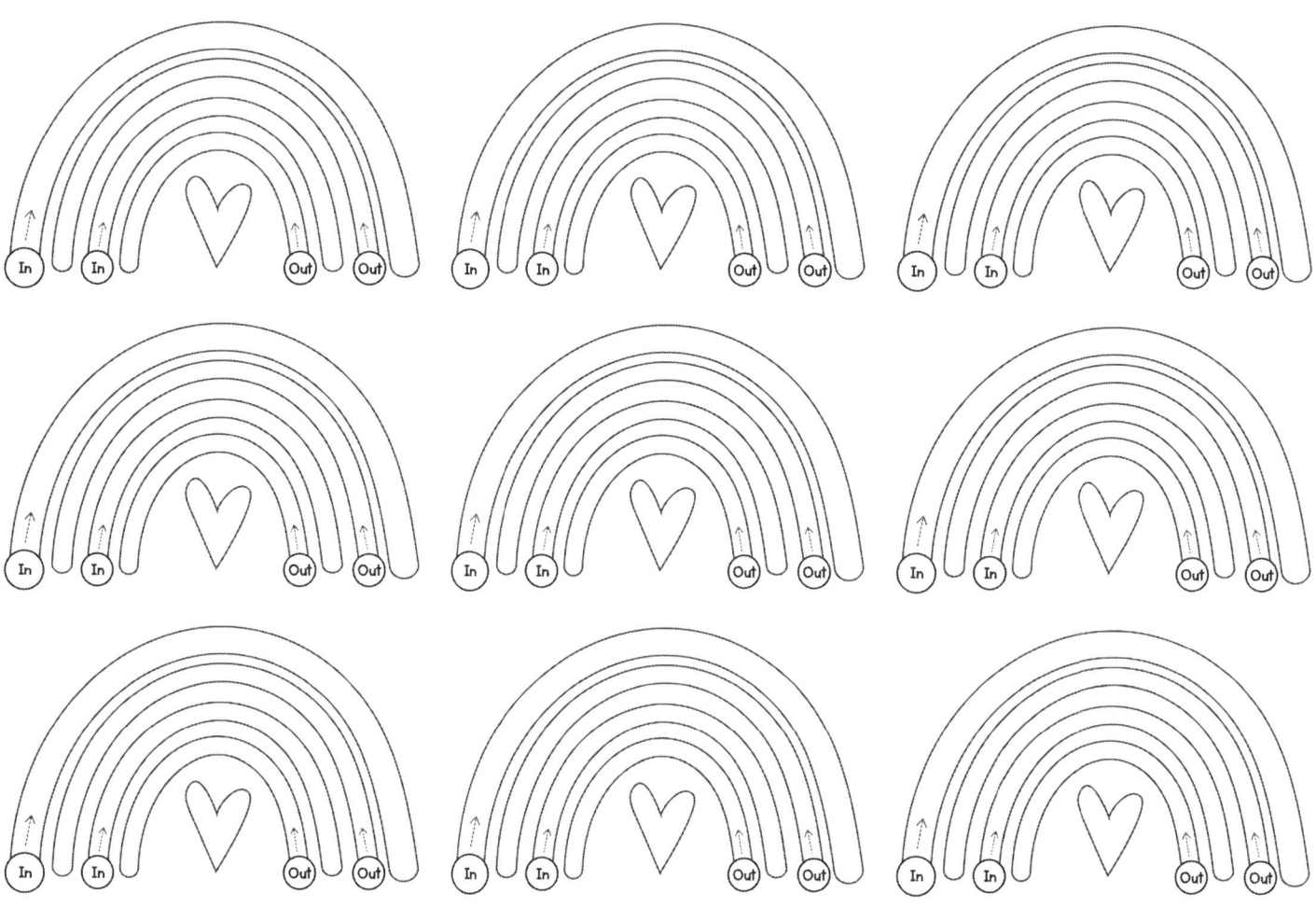

17

Rainbow Breathing

Directions:

With any drawing tool, trace the outer layer of the rainbow while breathing in. Then trace the inner layer of the rainbow while breathing out. Continue doing this until you feel calmer.

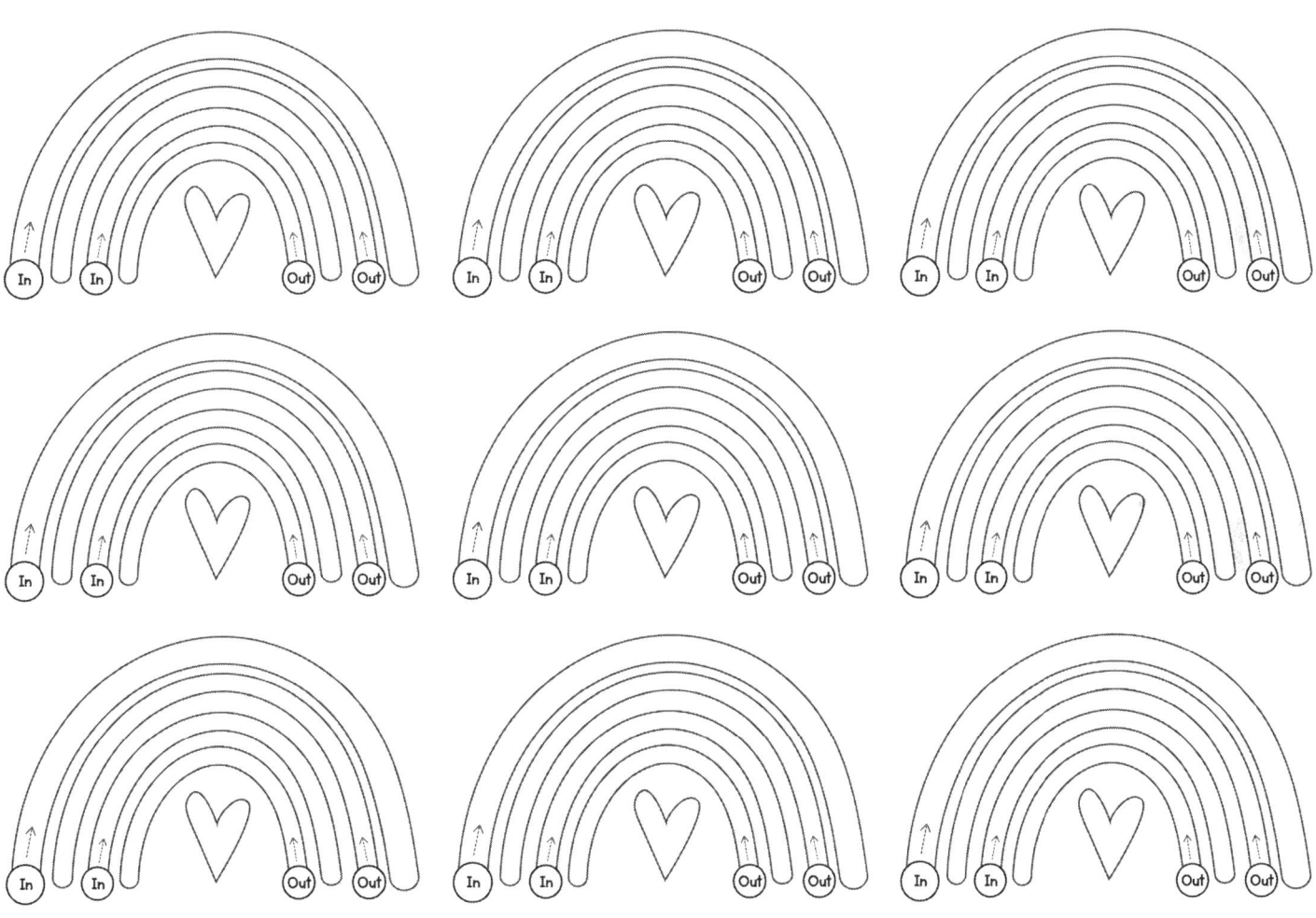

18

Spiral Breathing

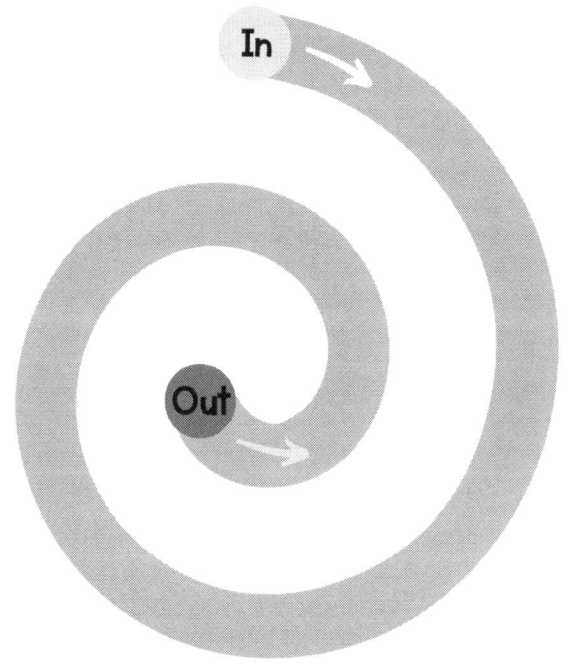

In

Out

Spiral Breathing

Directions:

Use your finger to trace the outline of the shape, breathe in. Then trace your finger back as you breathe out. Do this at least 5 times or until you feel calmer.

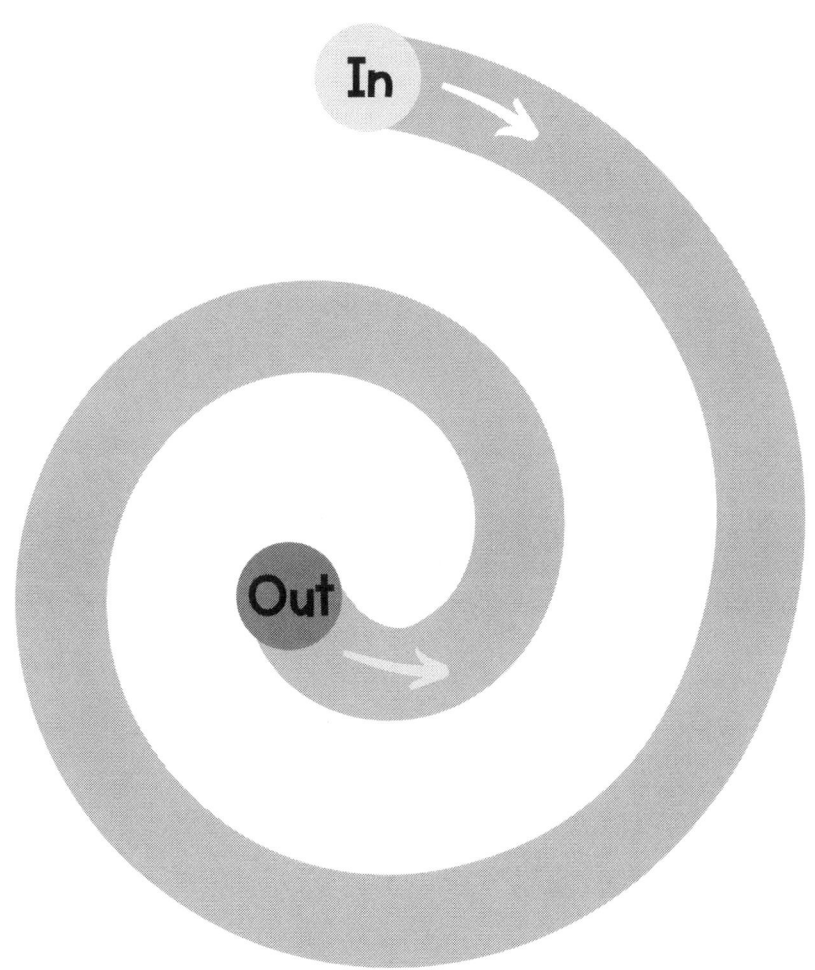

"Feelings come and go like clouds in a windy sky. Conscious breathing is my anchor."

- Thich Nhat Hanh

Spiral Breathing

Directions:
With any drawing tool, trace the outline of the shape as you breathe in. Then trace back along the same line as you breathe out. Continue this process at least 5 times or until you feel calmer.

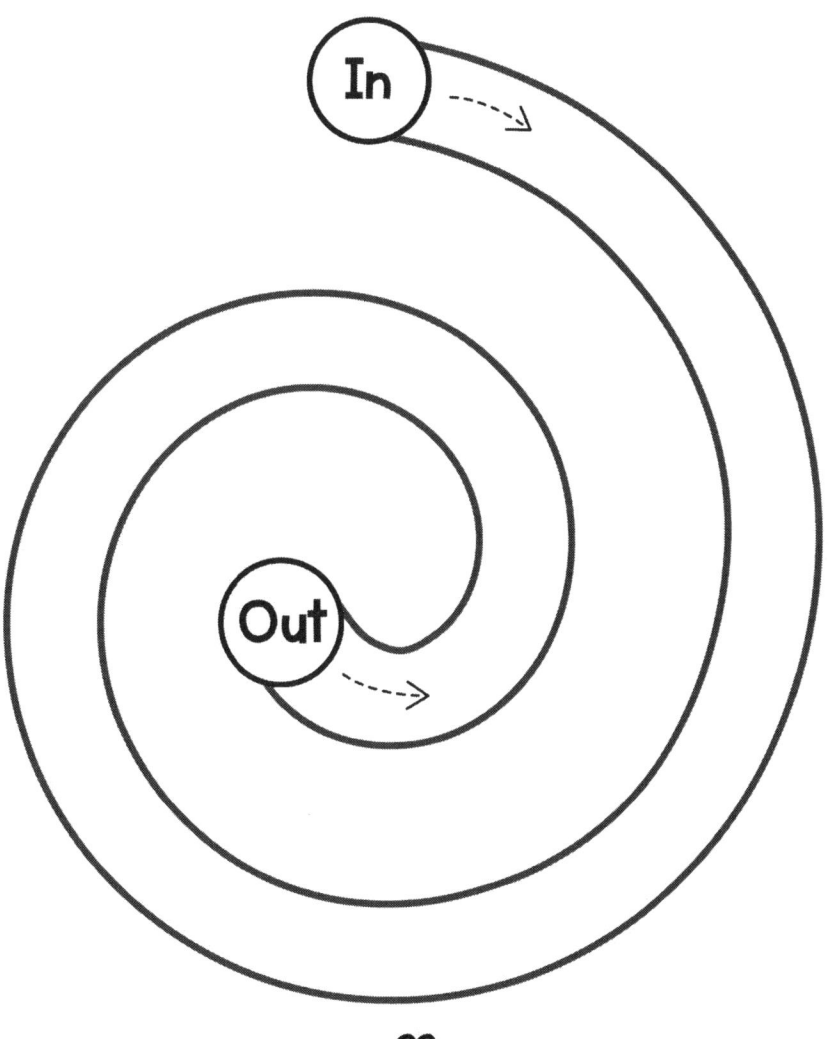

22

Spiral Breathing

With any drawing tool, trace the outline of the shape as you breathe in. Then trace back along the same line as you breathe out. Continue this process at least 5 times or until you feel calmer.

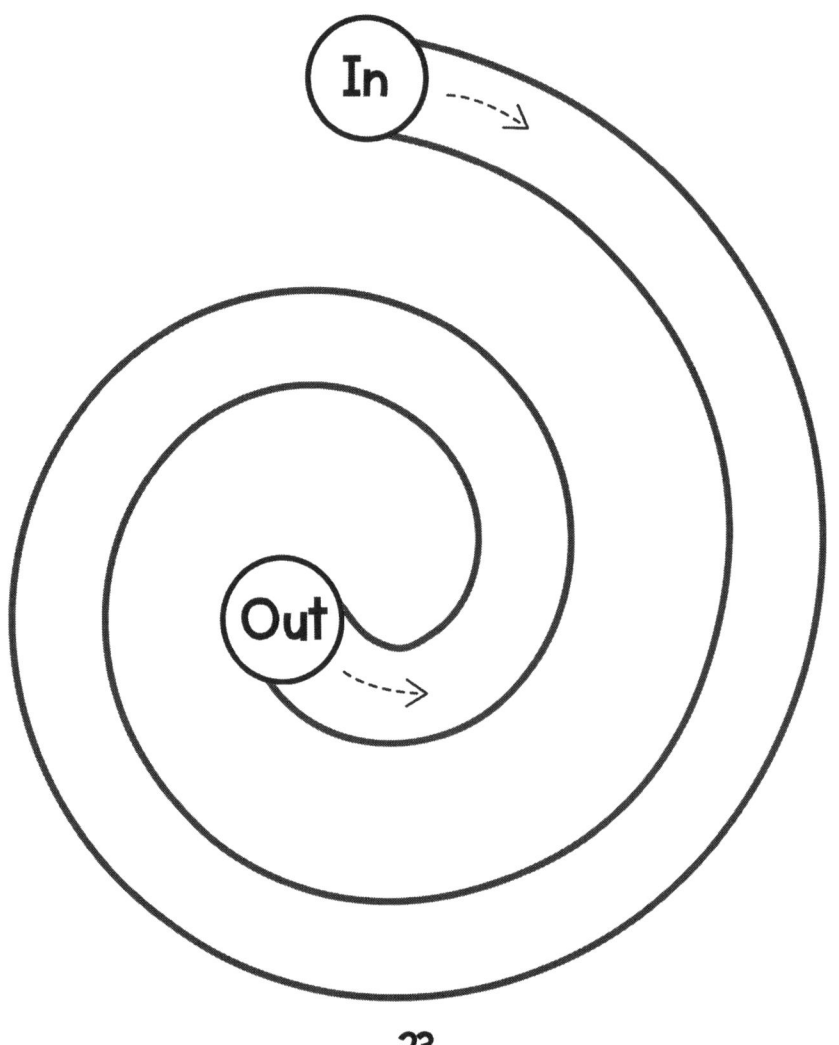

Spiral Breathing

Directions:

With any drawing tool, trace the outline of the shape as you breathe in. Then trace back along the same line as you breathe out. Continue this process at least 5 times or until you feel calmer.

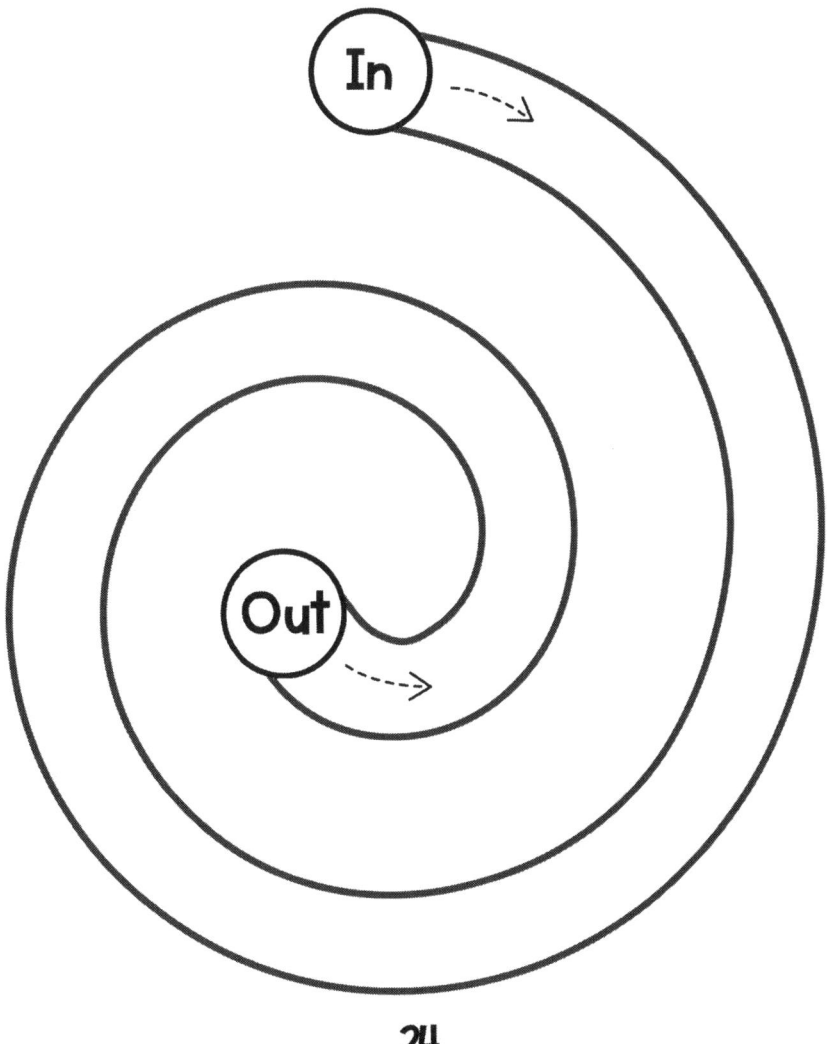

Spiral Breathing

Directions:

With any drawing tool, trace the outline of the shape as you breathe in. Then trace back along the same line as you breathe out. Continue this process until you feel calmer.

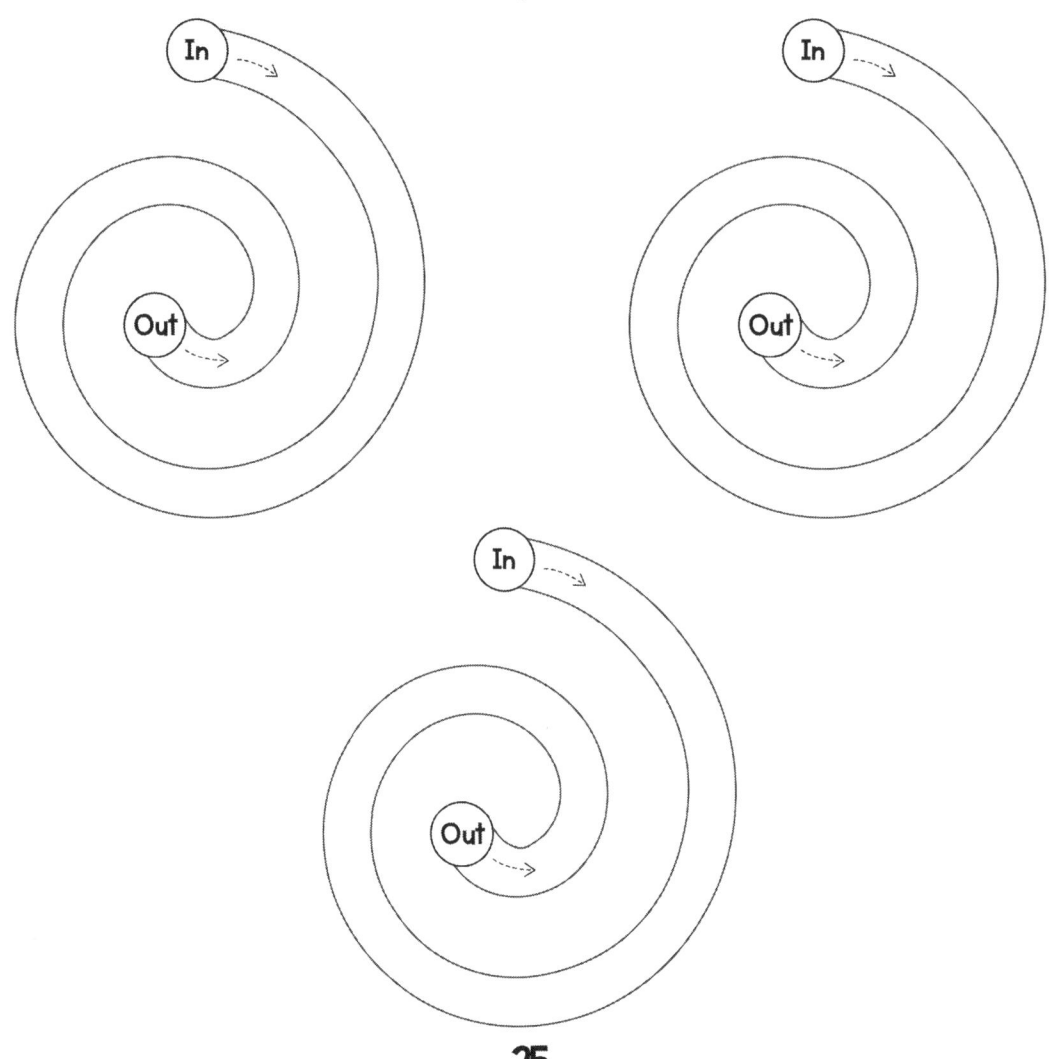

25

Spiral Breathing

Directions:

With any drawing tool, trace the outline of the shape as you breathe in. Then trace back along the same line as you breathe out. Continue this process until you feel calmer.

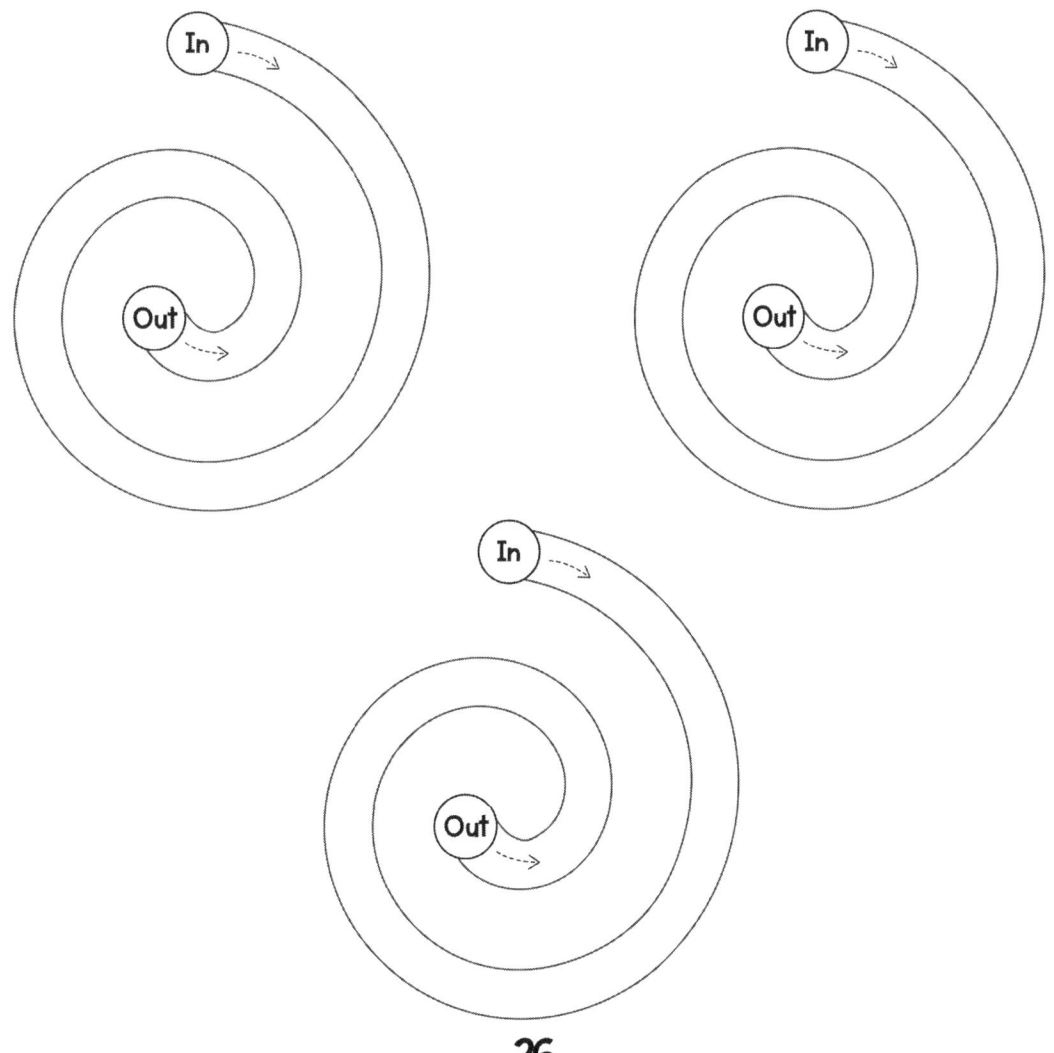

26

Spiral Breathing

Directions:

With any drawing tool, trace the outline of the shape as you breathe in. Then trace back along the same line as you breathe out. Continue this process until you feel calmer.

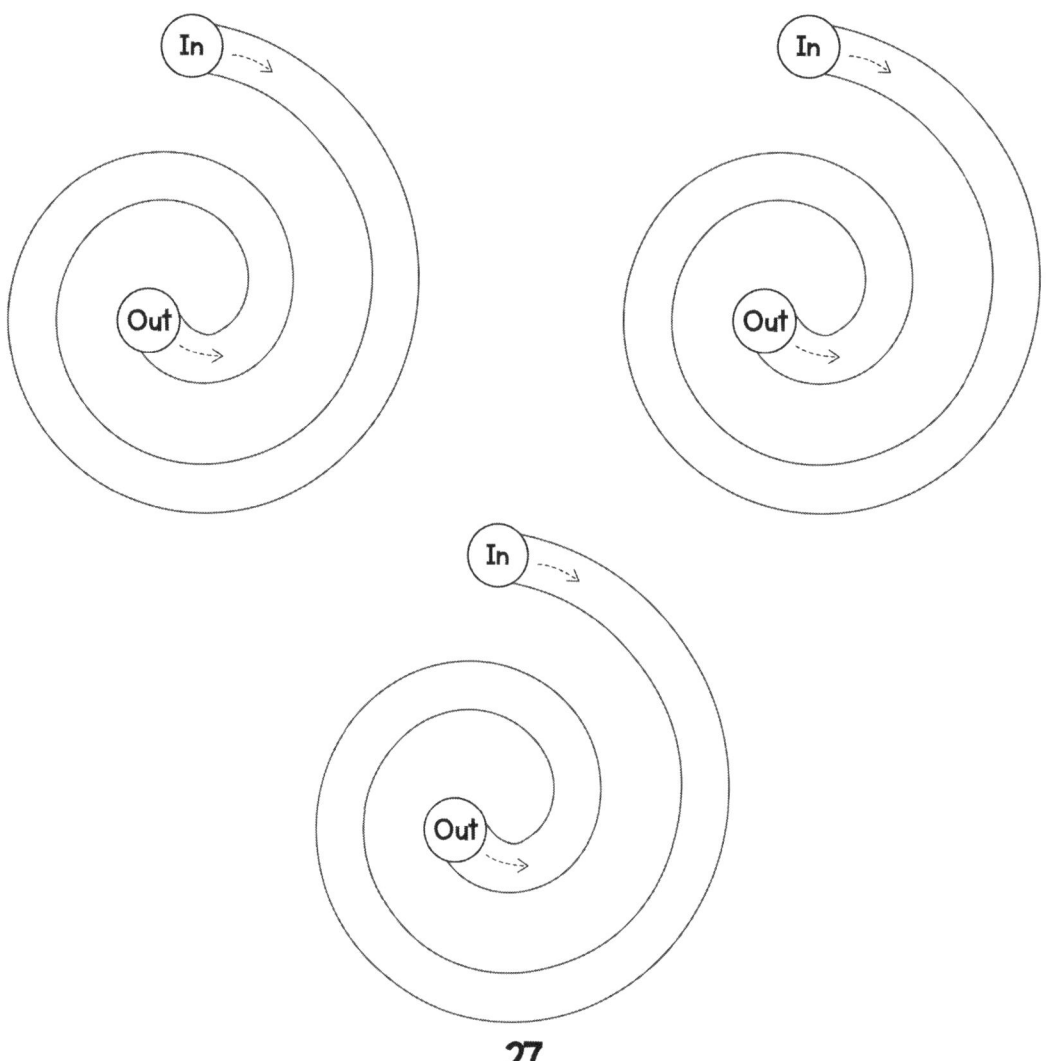

Spiral Breathing

Directions:

With any drawing tool, trace the outline of the shape as you breathe in. Then trace back along the same line as you breathe out. Continue this process until you feel calmer.

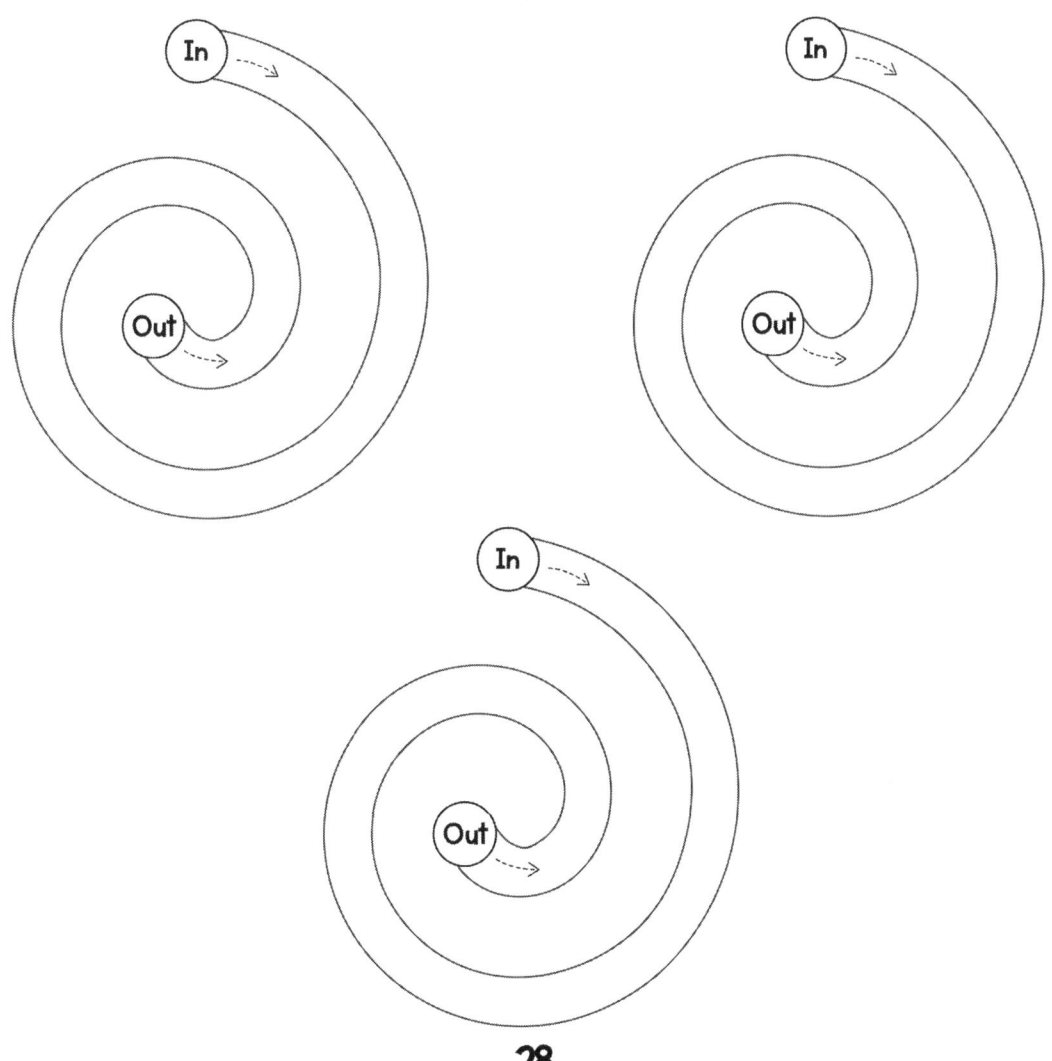

28

Spiral Breathing

Directions:

With any drawing tool, trace the outline of the shape as you breathe in. Then trace back along the same line as you breathe out. Continue this process until you feel calmer.

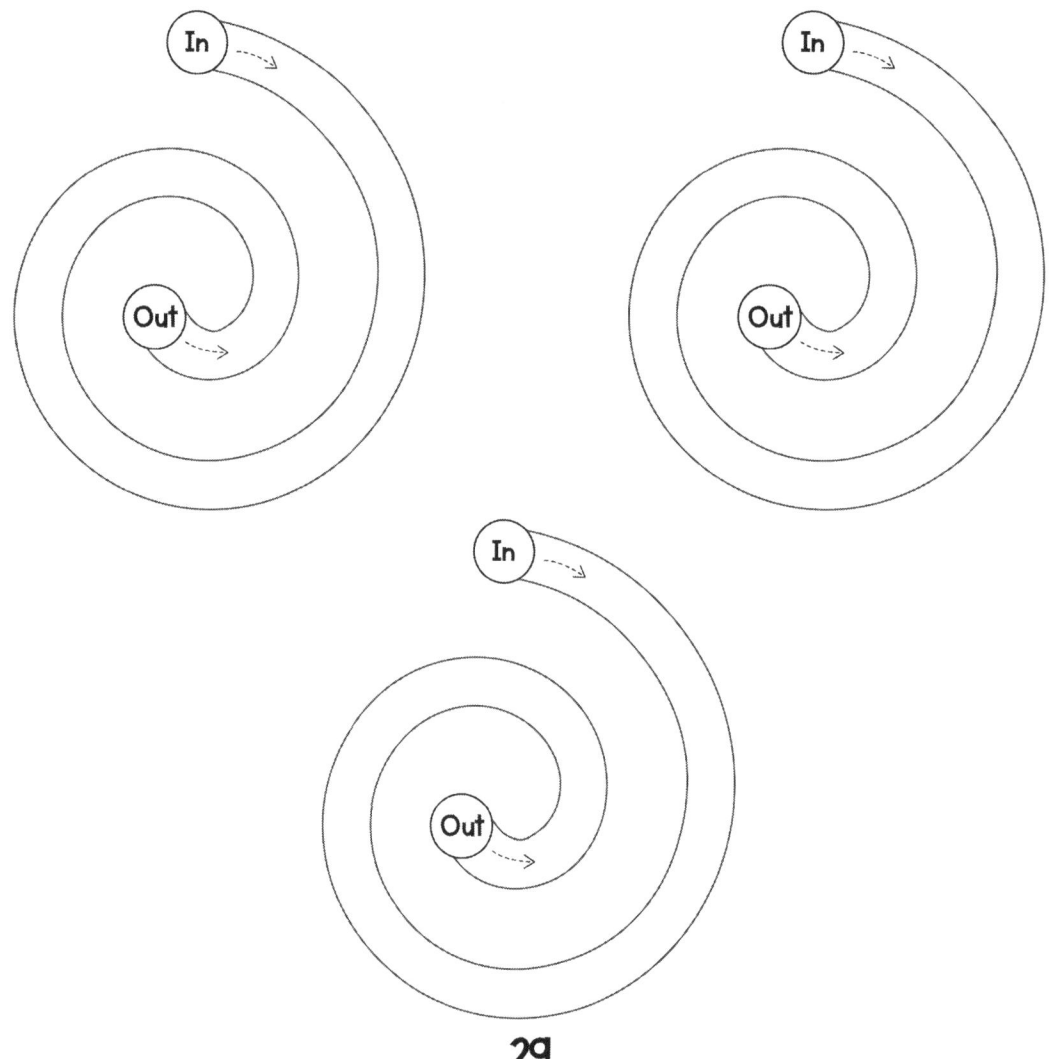

Spiral Breathing

Directions:

With any drawing tool, trace the outline of the shape as you breathe in. Then trace back along the same line as you breathe out. Continue this process until you feel calmer.

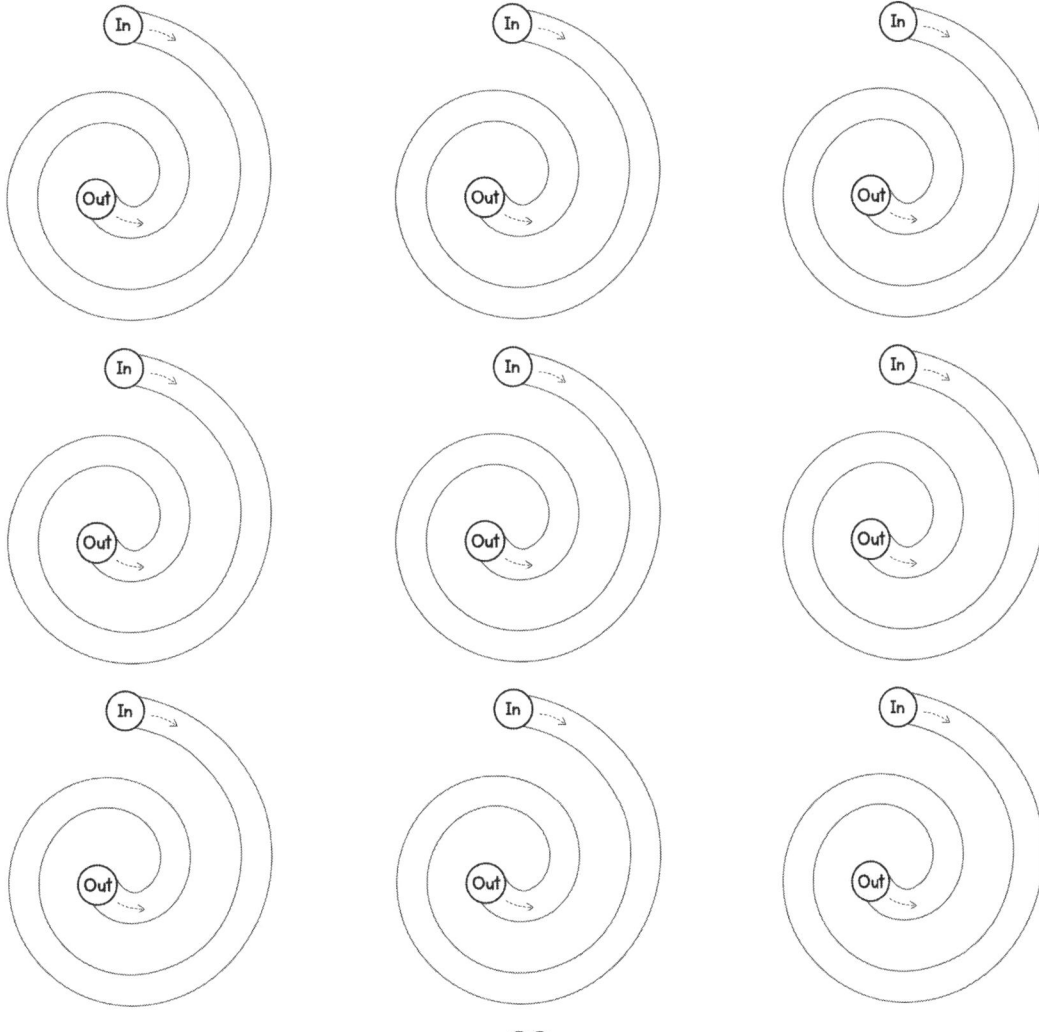

Spiral Breathing

Directions:

With any drawing tool, trace the outline of the shape as you breathe in. Then trace back along the same line as you breathe out. Continue this process until you feel calmer.

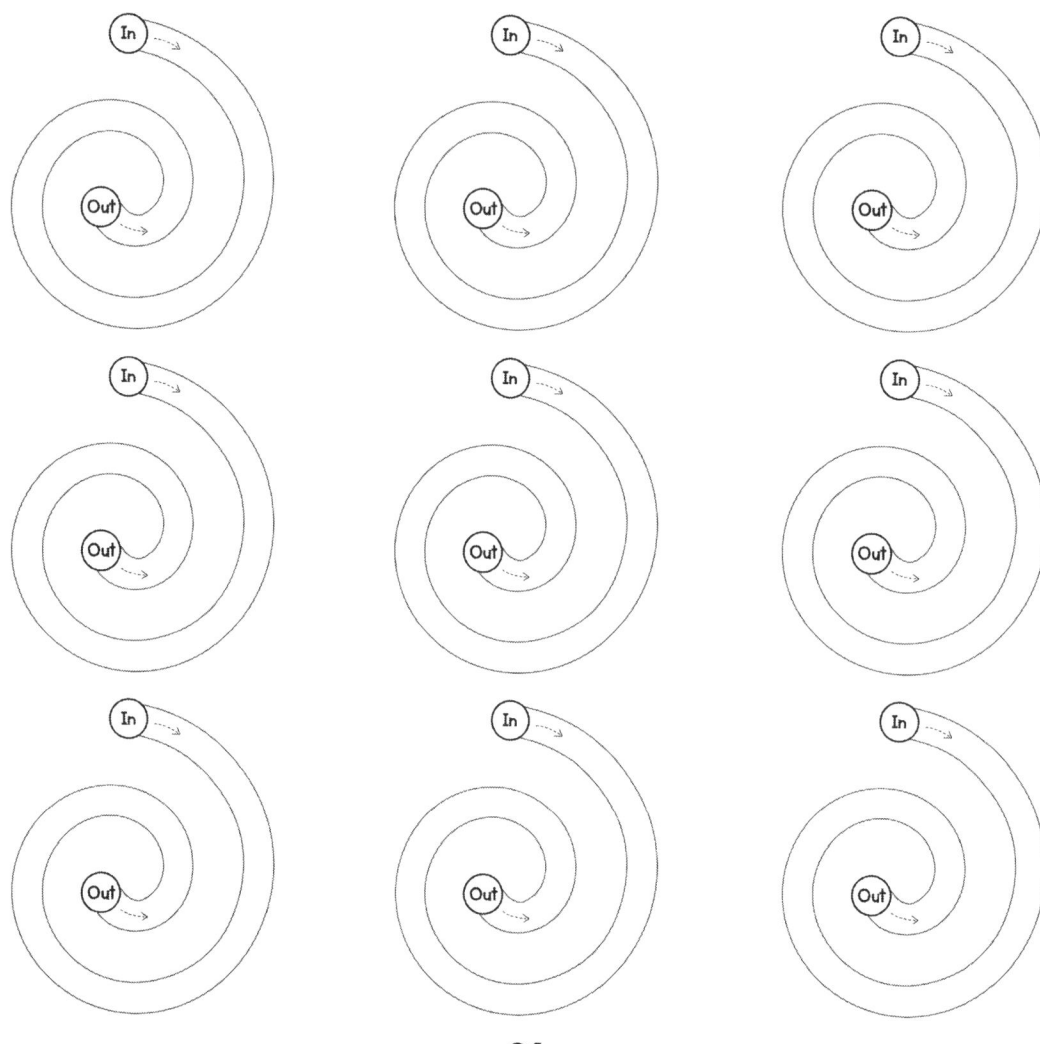

Spiral Breathing

Directions:

With any drawing tool, trace the outline of the shape as you breathe in. Then trace back along the same line as you breathe out. Continue this process until you feel calmer.

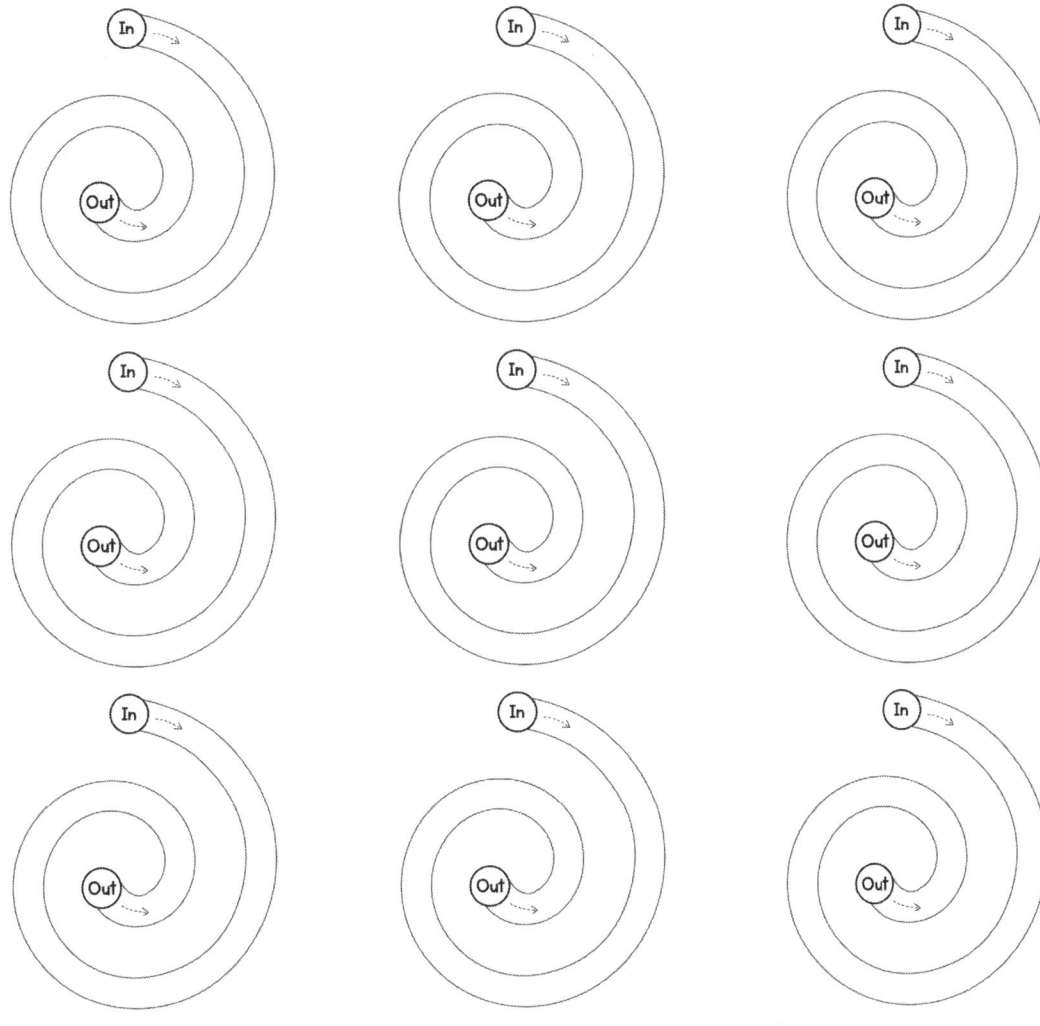

32

Spiral Breathing

Directions:

With any drawing tool, trace the outline of the shape as you breathe in. Then trace back along the same line as you breathe out. Continue this process until you feel calmer.

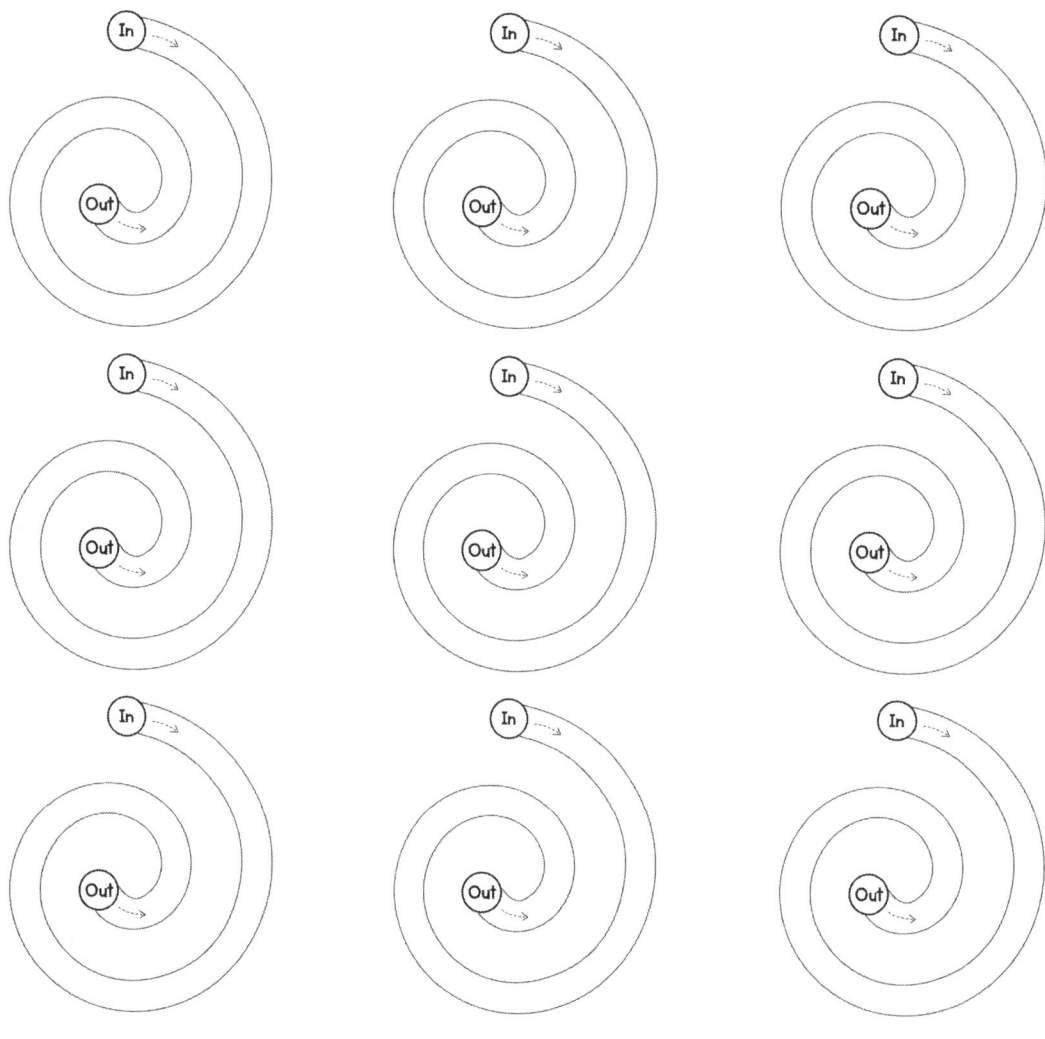

33

Spiral Breathing

With any drawing tool, trace the outline of the shape as you breathe in. Then trace back along the same line as you breathe out. Continue this process until you feel calmer.

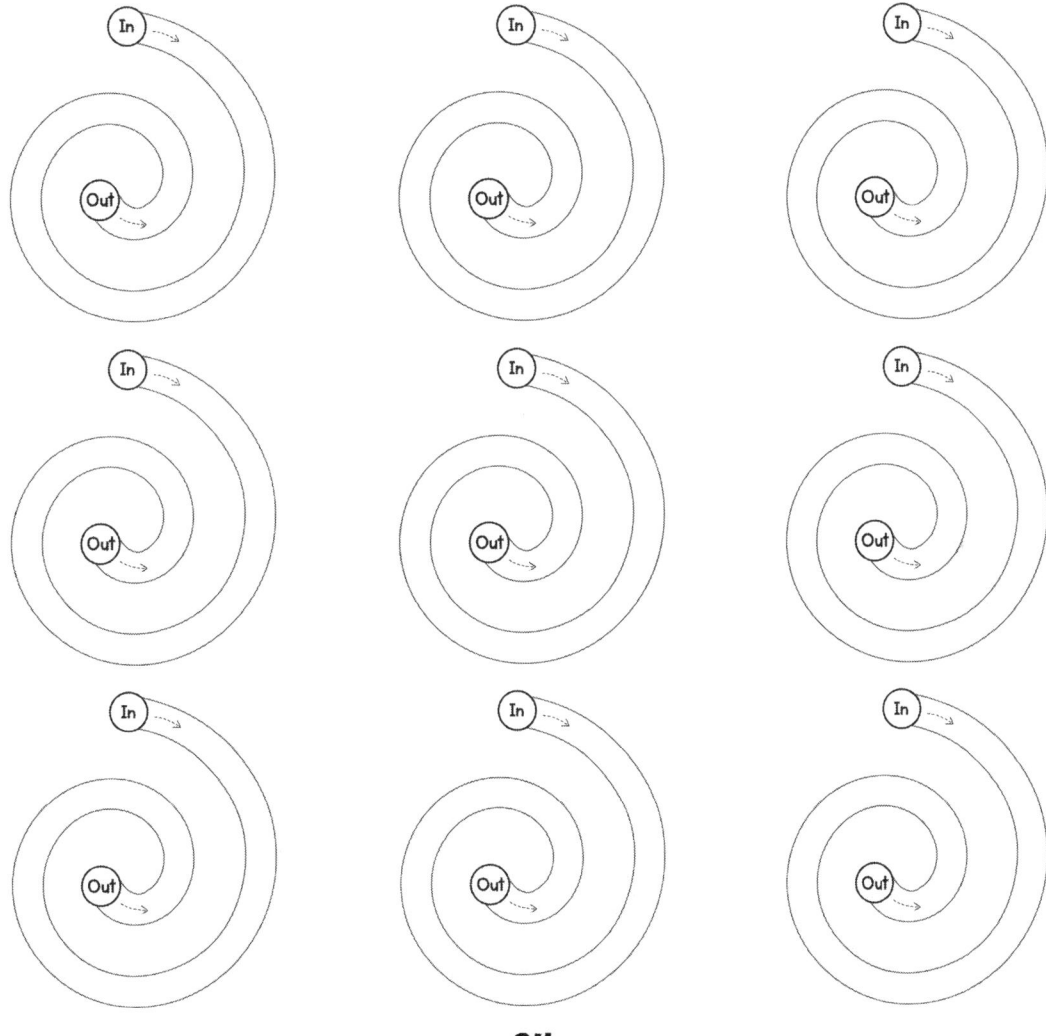

34

Triangle Breathing

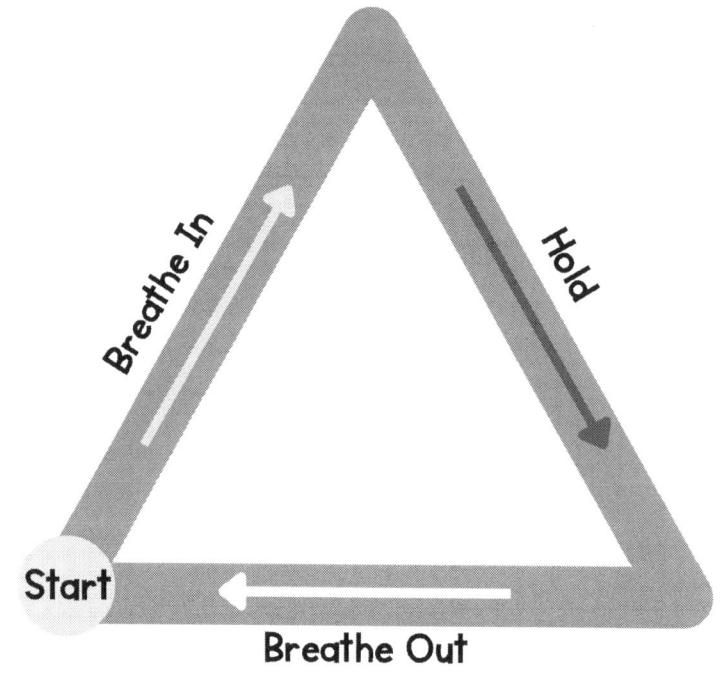

Triangle Breathing

Directions:
Use your finger to trace the outline of the shape, breathe in, hold your breath, and breathe out as you go. Do this for at least 5 times or until you feel calmer.

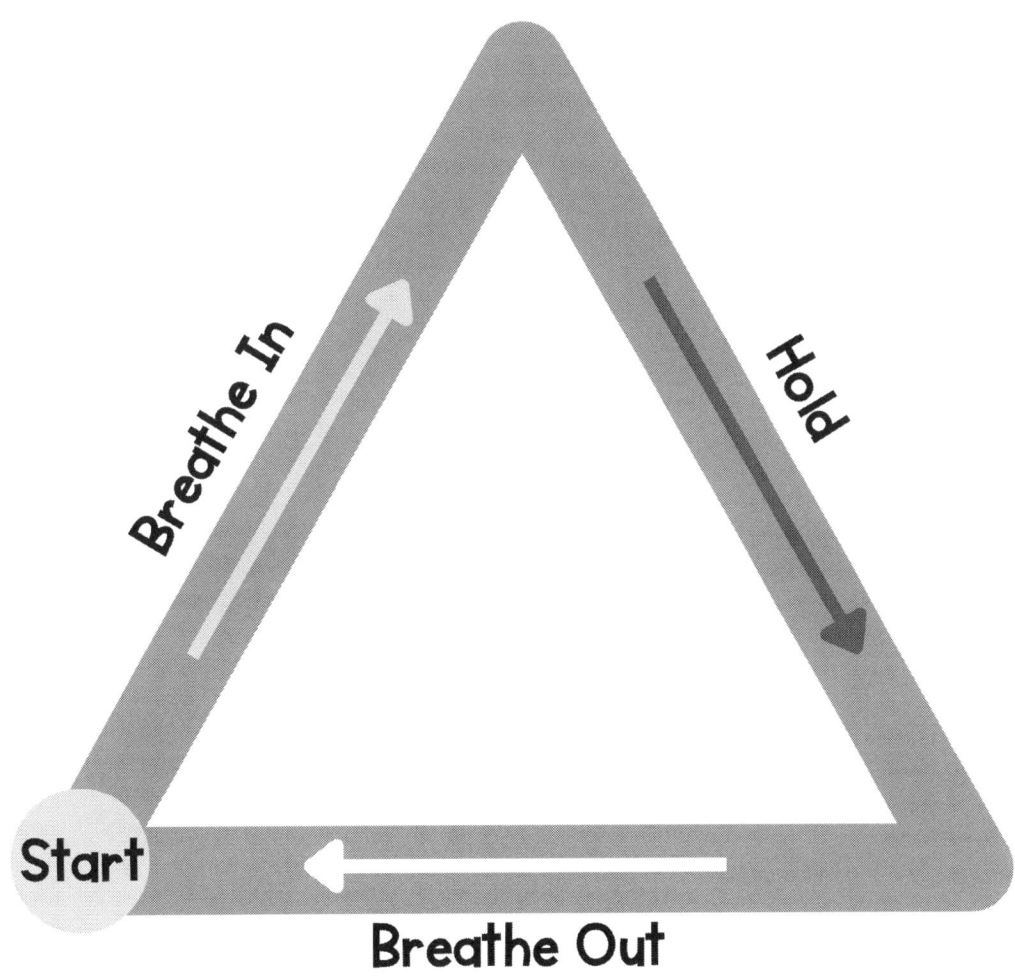

36

"Just keep swimming. Just keep swimming."

- Dory in 'Finding Nemo'

Triangle Breathing

Directions:

With any drawing tool, trace the outline of the shape. As you do, breathe in, hold your breath, and then breathe out. Repeat this process at least 5 times or until you feel calmer.

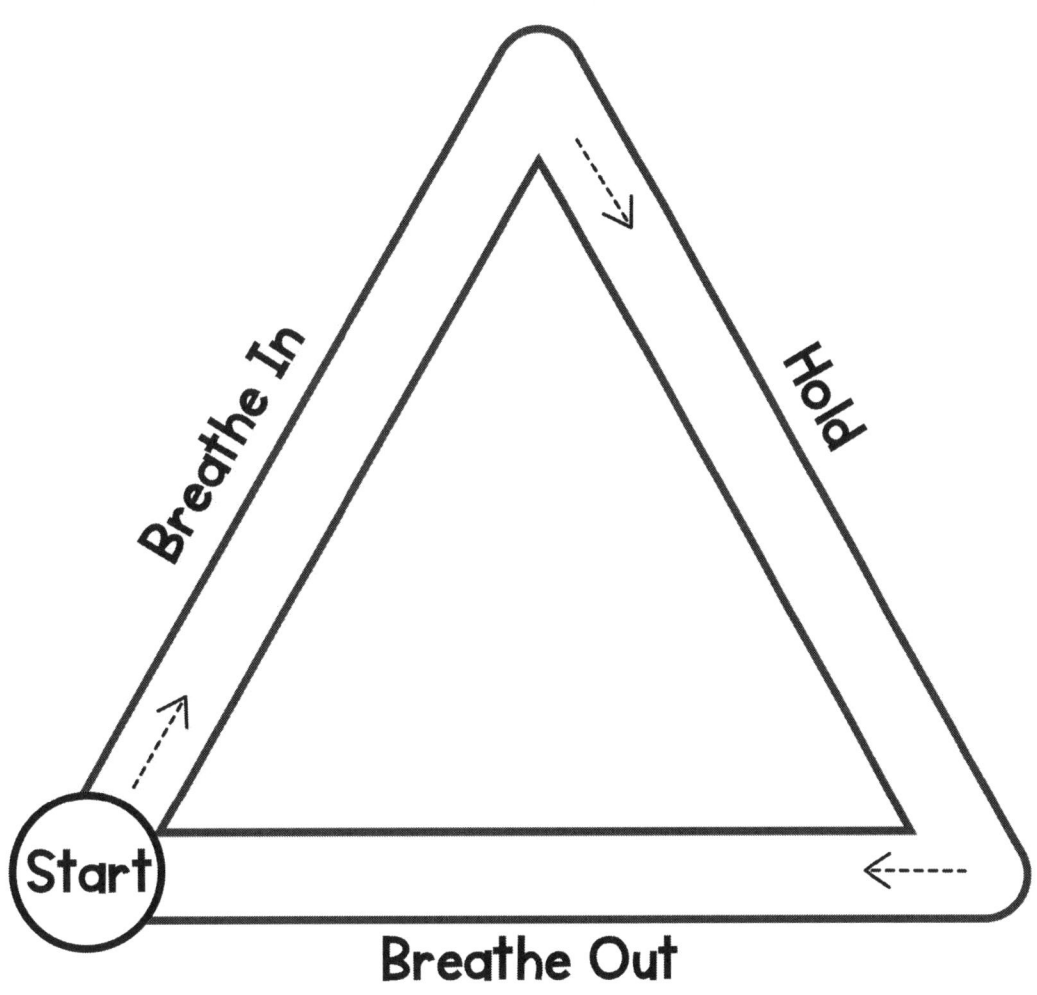

38

Triangle Breathing

Directions:
With any drawing tool, trace the outline of the shape. As you do, breathe in, hold your breath, and then breathe out. Repeat this process at least 5 times or until you feel calmer.

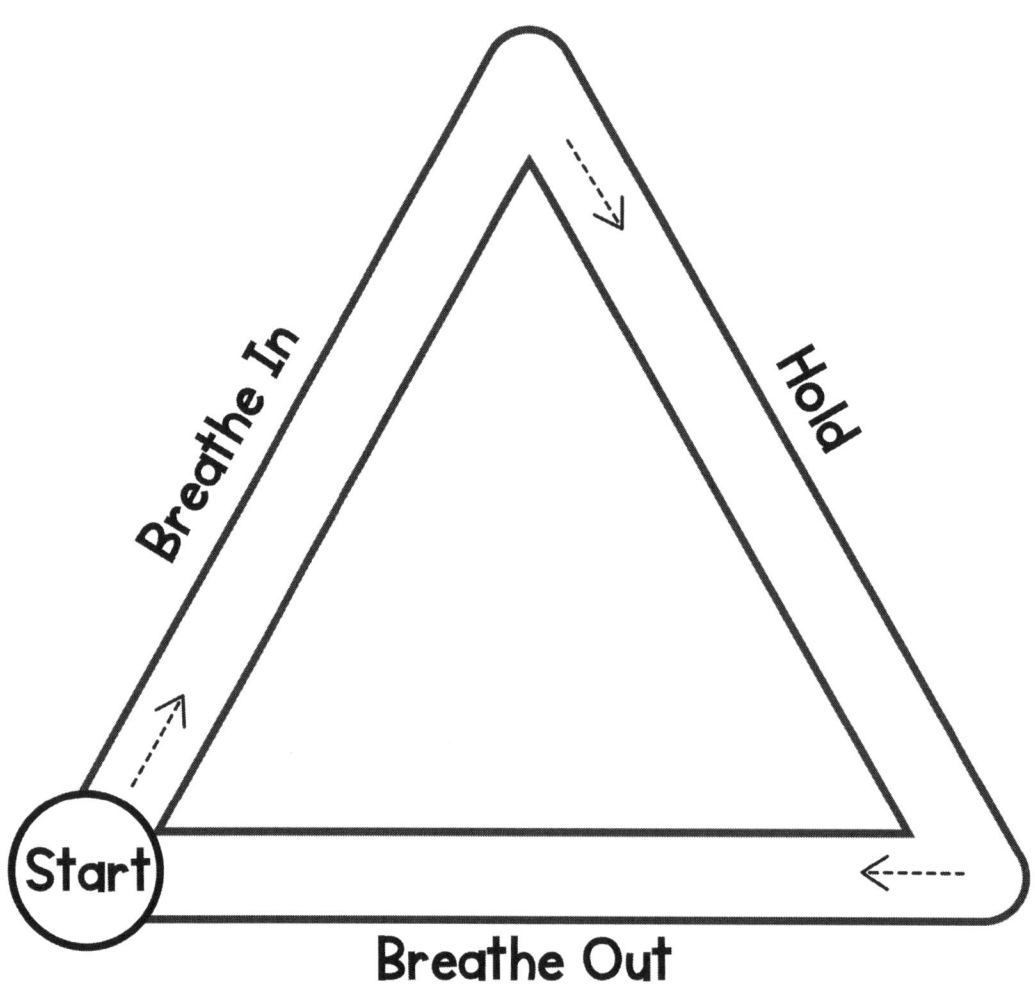

39

Triangle Breathing

Directions:
With any drawing tool, trace the outline of the shape. As you do, breathe in, hold your breath, and then breathe out. Repeat this process at least 5 times or until you feel calmer.

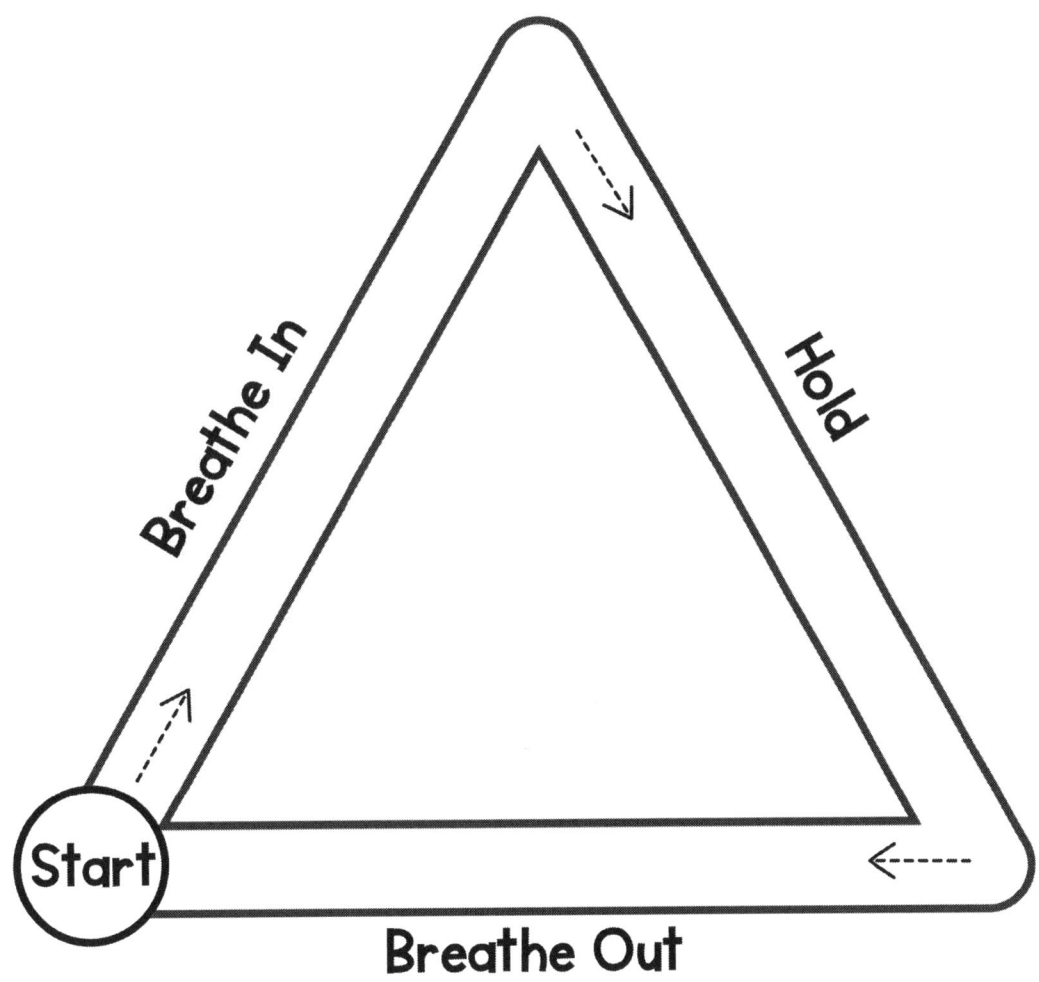

Triangle Breathing

Directions:

With any drawing tool, trace the outline of the shape. As you do, breathe in, hold your breath, and then breathe out. Repeat this process until you feel calmer.

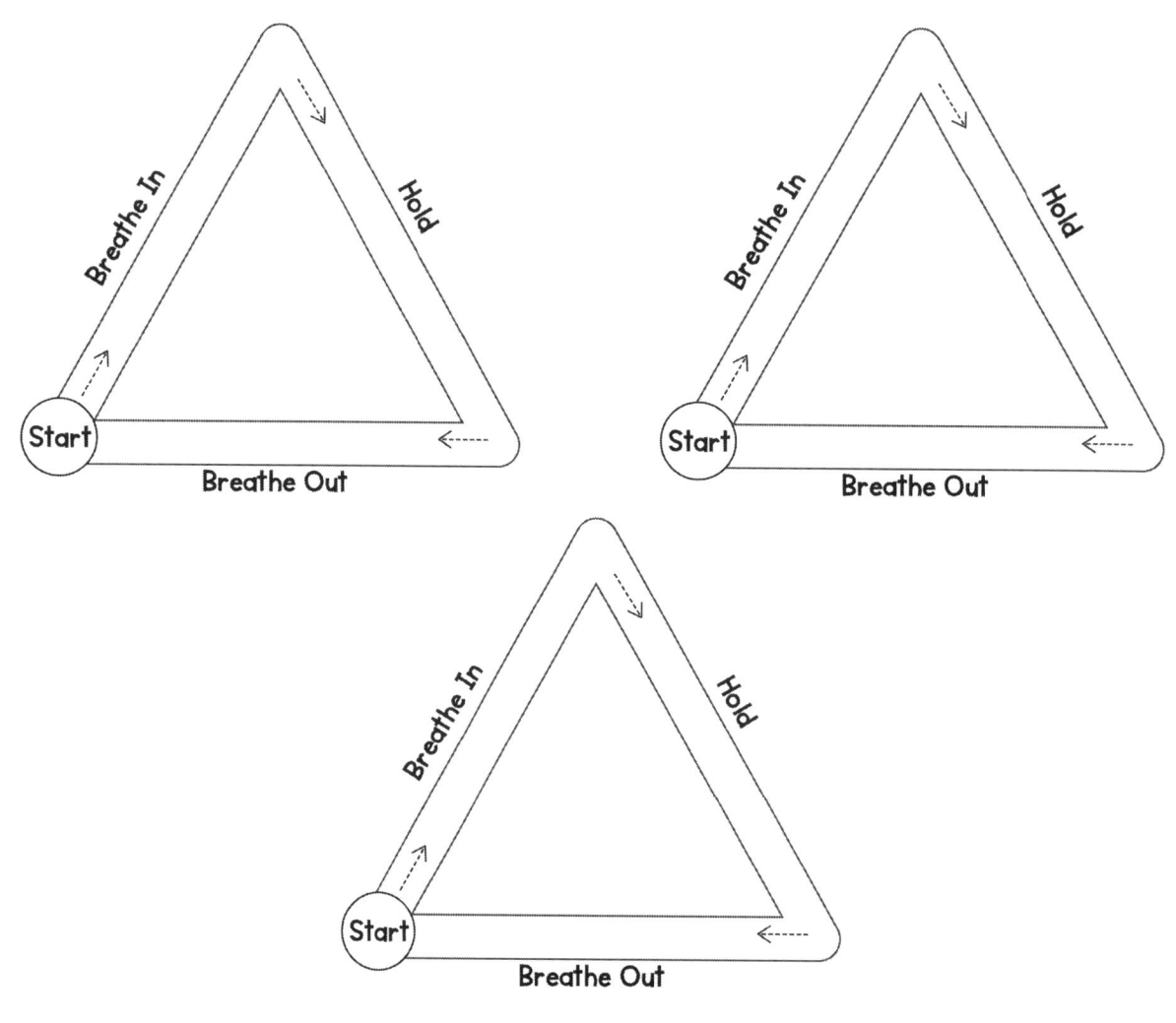

Triangle Breathing

Directions:

With any drawing tool, trace the outline of the shape. As you do, breathe in, hold your breath, and then breathe out. Repeat this process until you feel calmer.

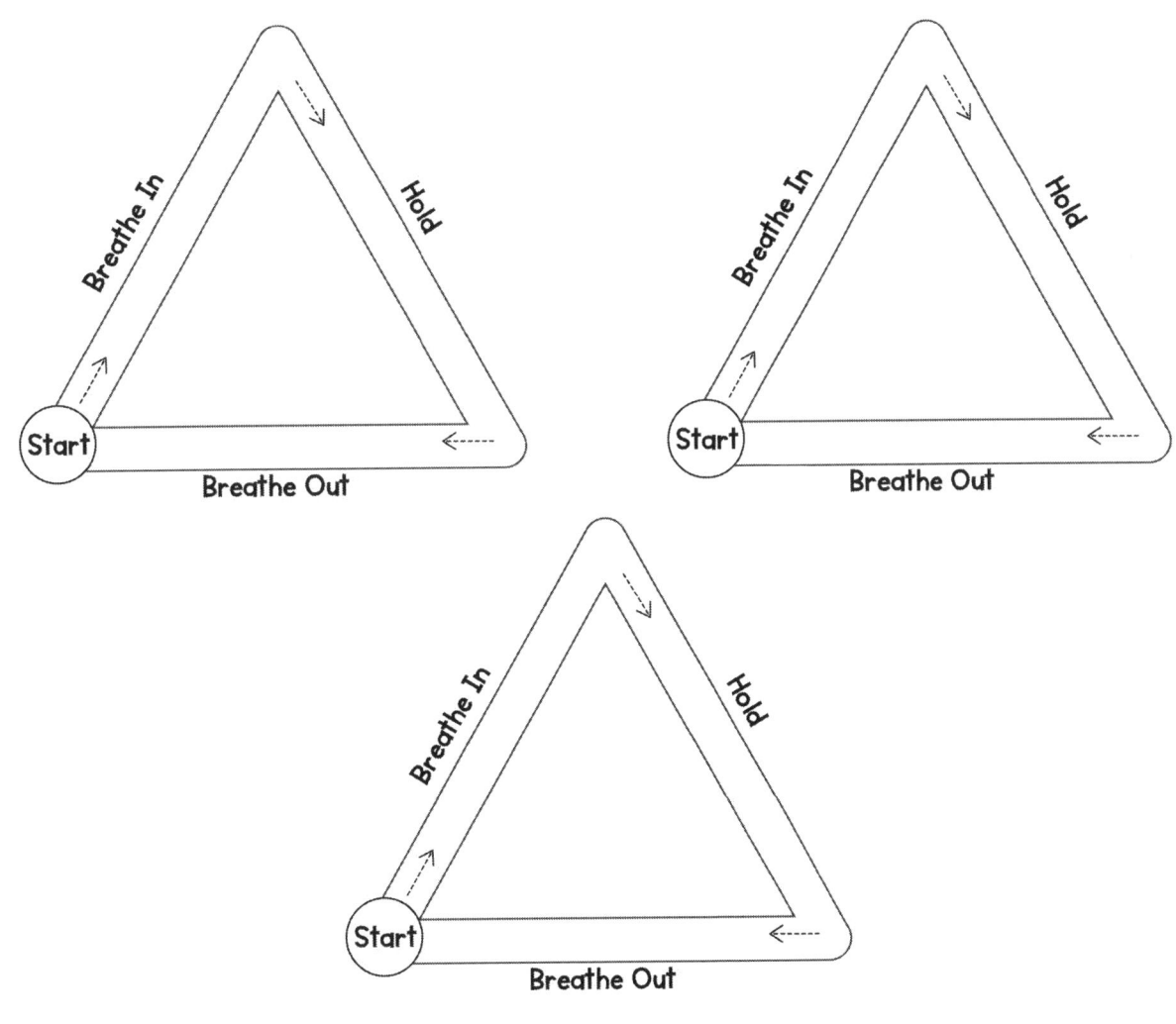

42

Triangle Breathing

Directions:

With any drawing tool, trace the outline of the shape. As you do, breathe in, hold your breath, and then breathe out. Repeat this process until you feel calmer.

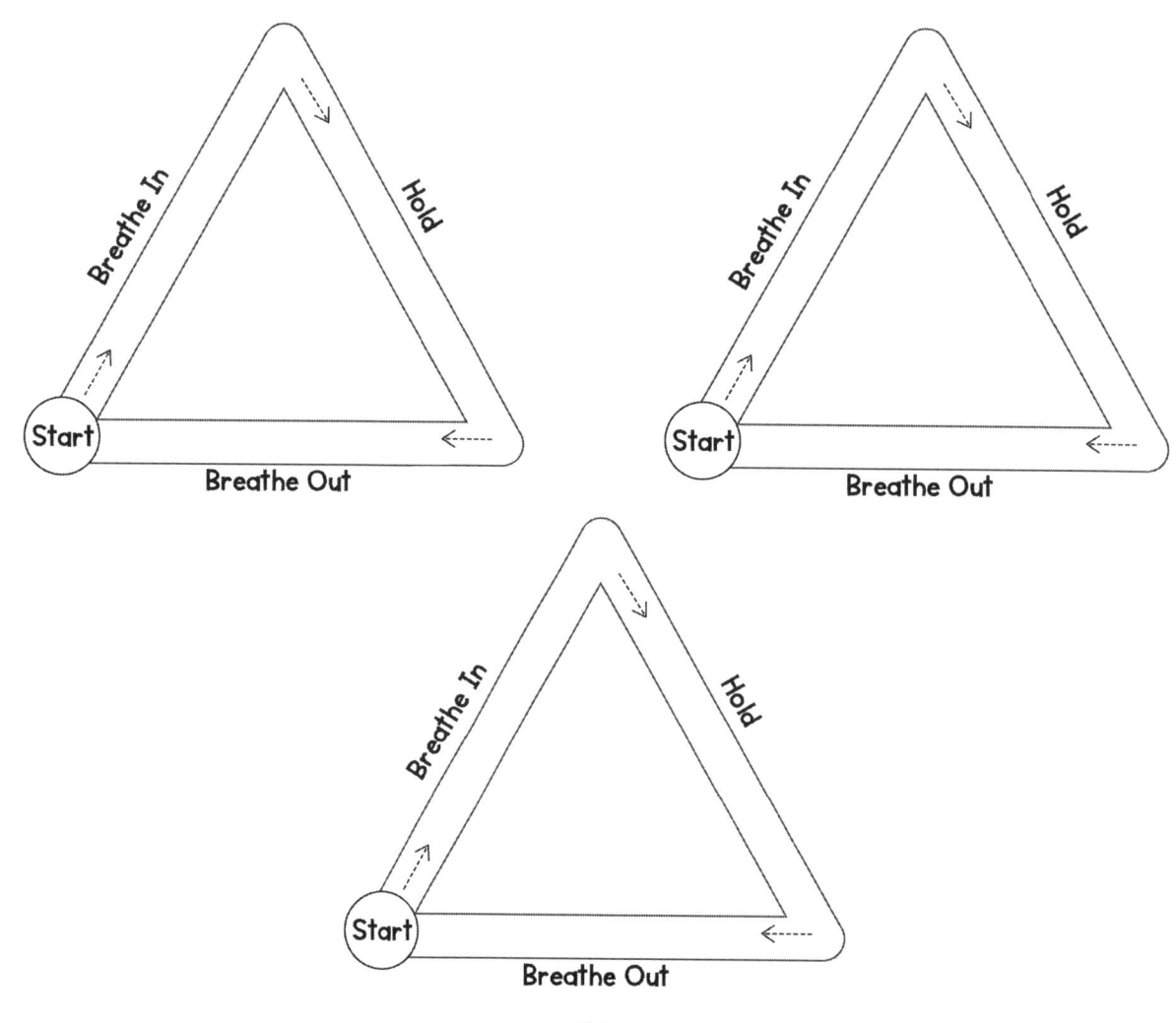

43

Triangle Breathing

Directions:

With any drawing tool, trace the outline of the shape. As you do, breathe in, hold your breath, and then breathe out. Repeat this process until you feel calmer.

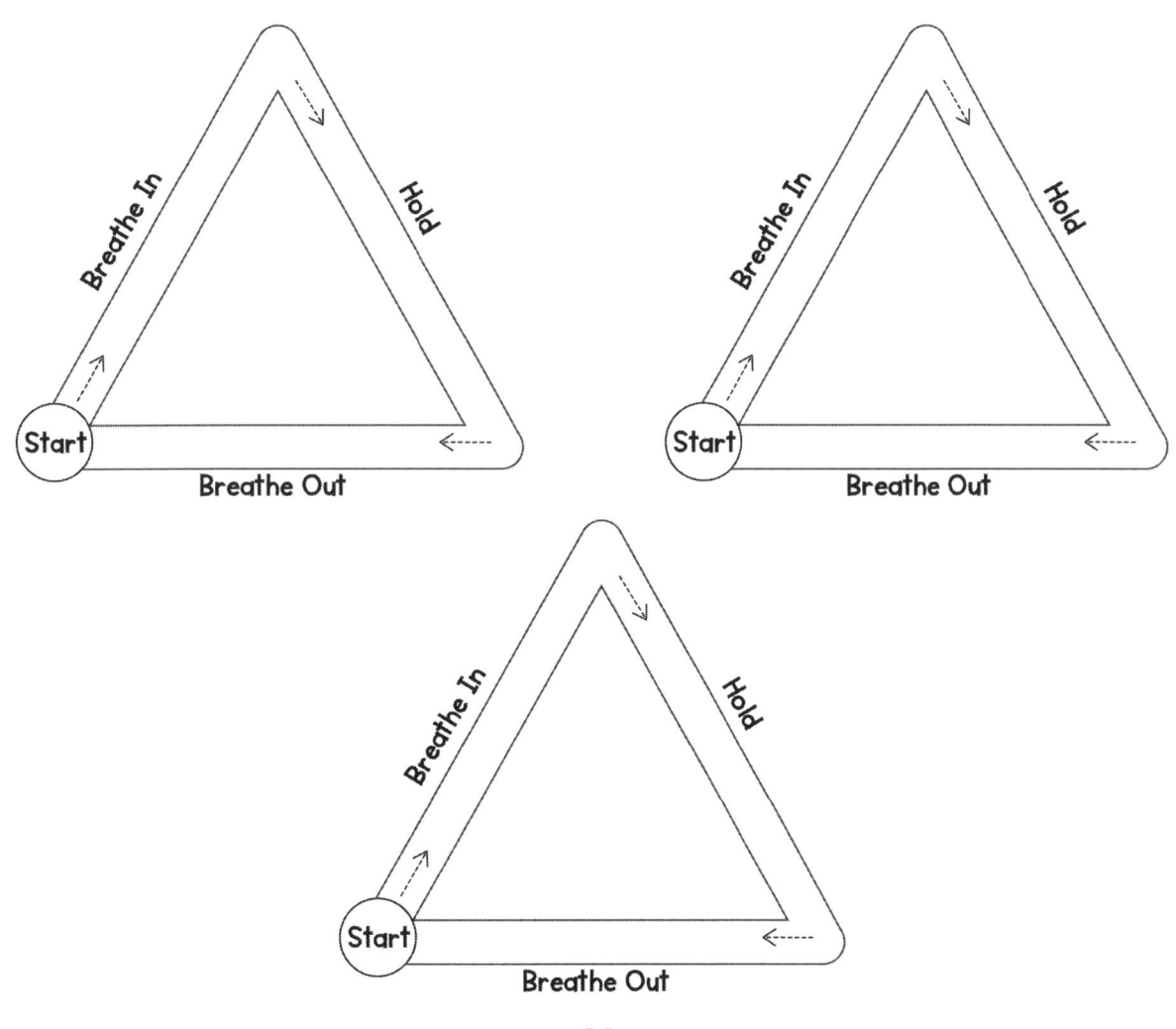

44

Triangle Breathing

Directions:

With any drawing tool, trace the outline of the shape. As you do, breathe in, hold your breath, and then breathe out. Repeat this process until you feel calmer.

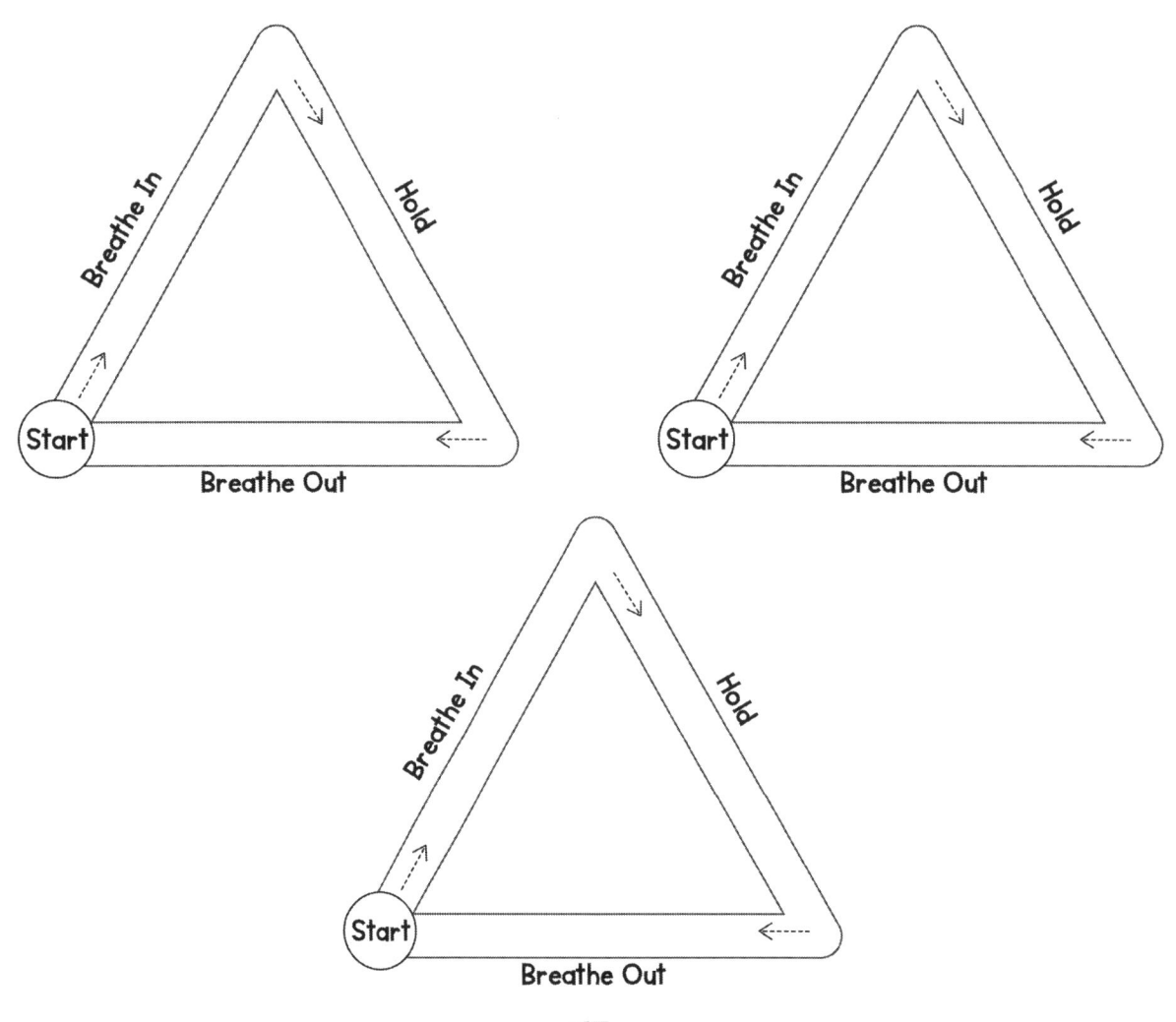

45

Triangle Breathing

Directions:

With any drawing tool, trace the outline of the shape. As you do, breathe in, hold your breath, and then breathe out. Repeat this process until you feel calmer.

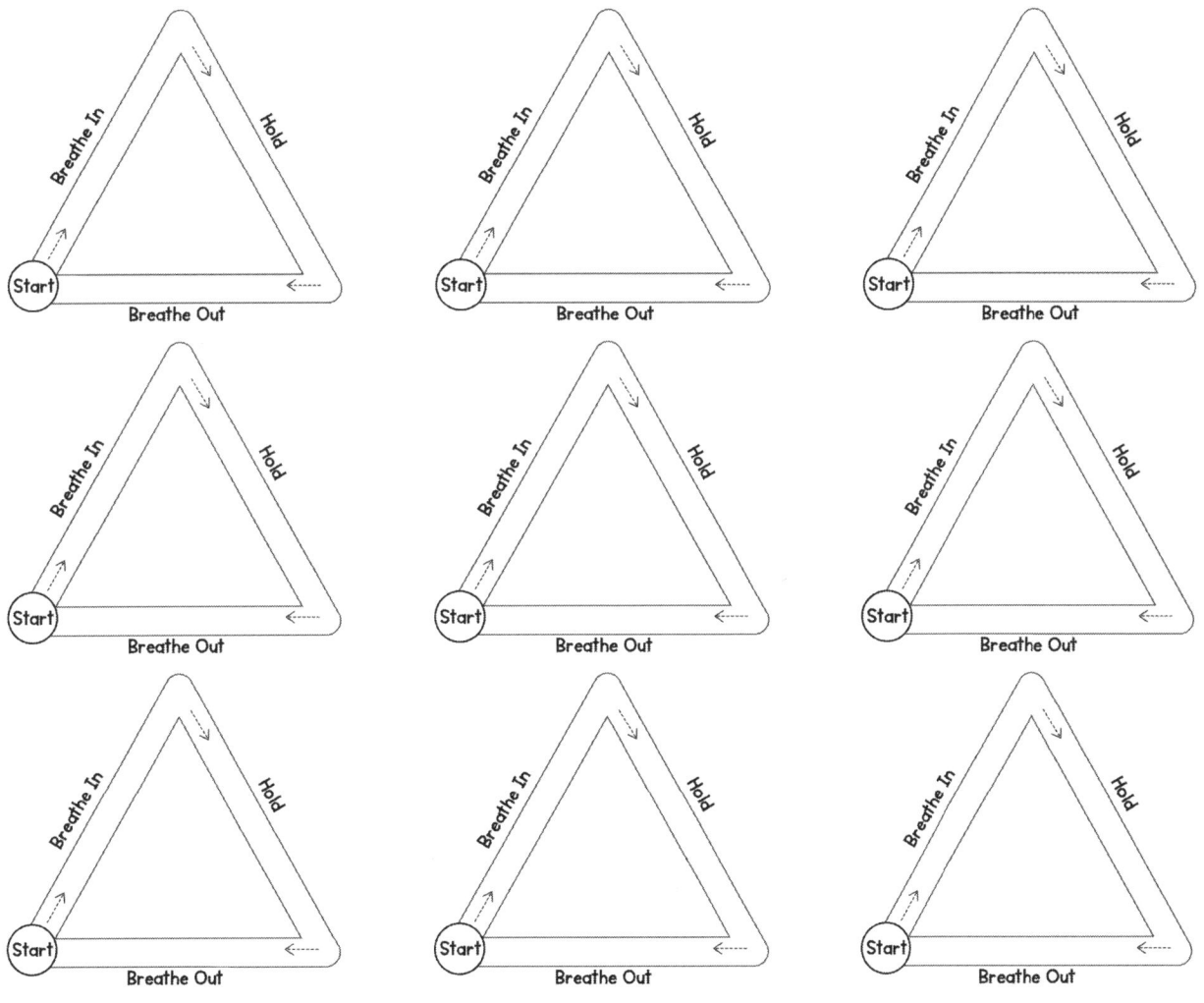

Triangle Breathing

Directions:

With any drawing tool, trace the outline of the shape. As you do, breathe in, hold your breath, and then breathe out. Repeat this process until you feel calmer.

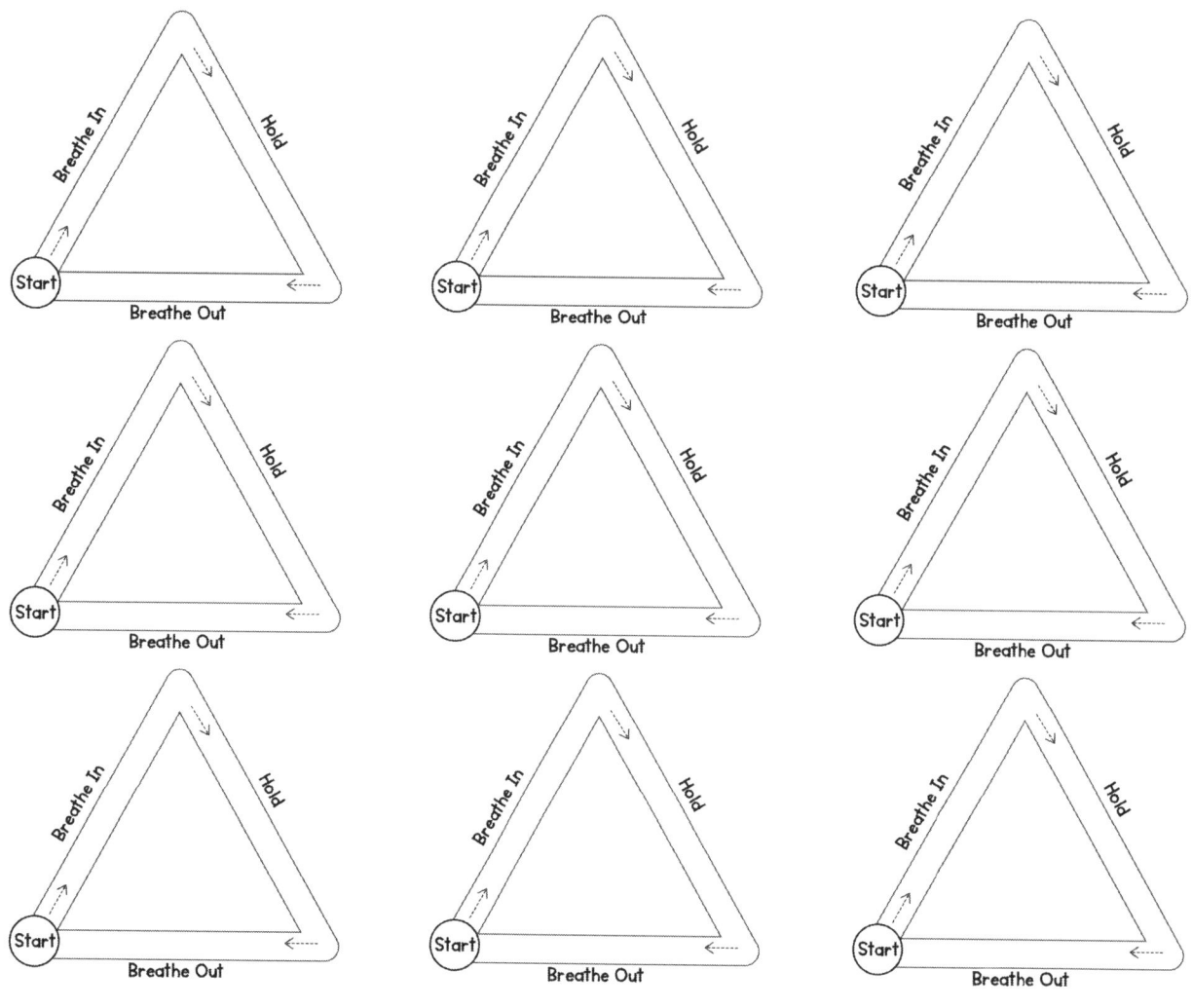

47

Triangle Breathing

Directions:

With any drawing tool, trace the outline of the shape. As you do, breathe in, hold your breath, and then breathe out. Repeat this process until you feel calmer.

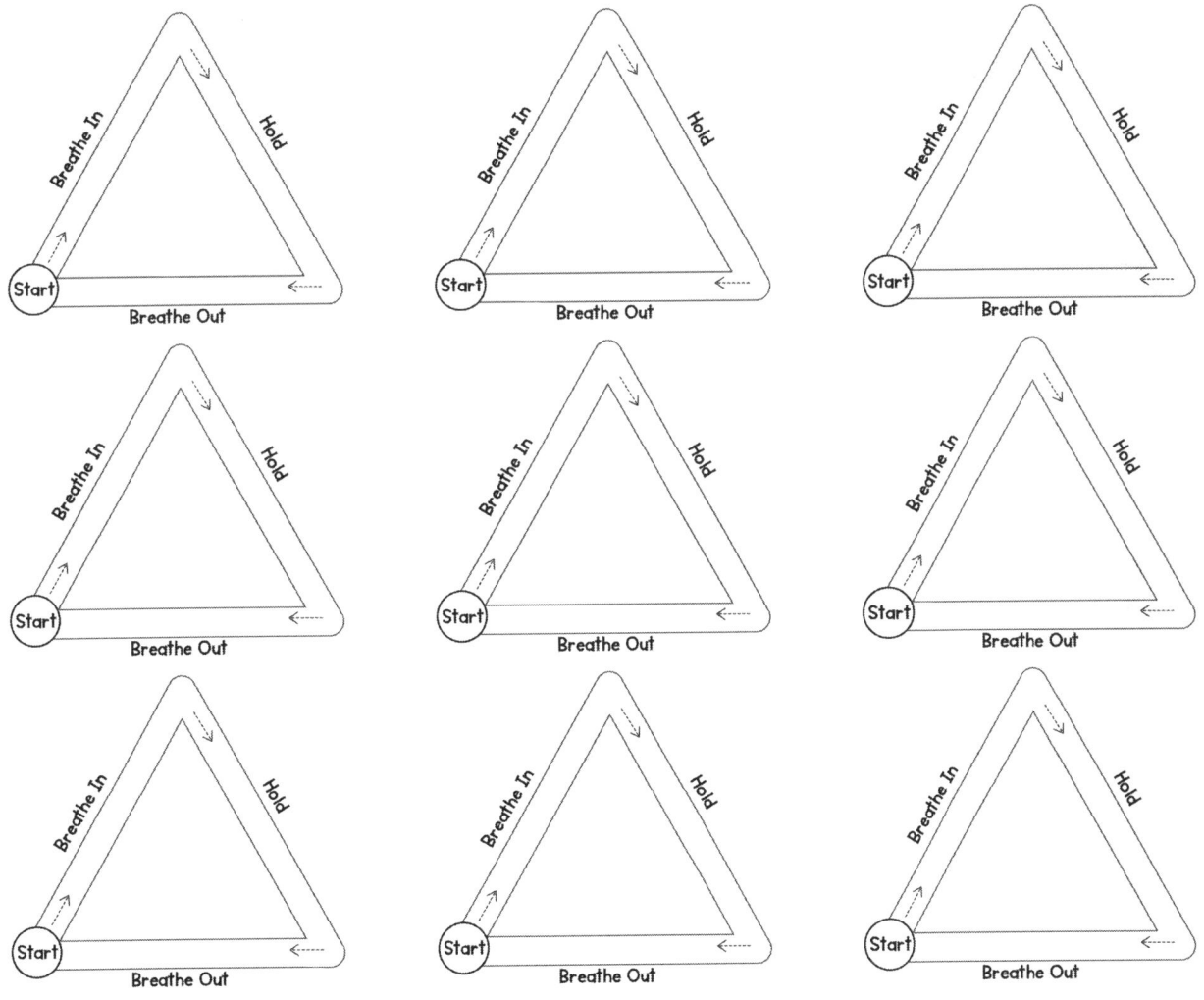

48

Triangle Breathing

Directions:

With any drawing tool, trace the outline of the shape. As you do, breathe in, hold your breath, and then breathe out. Repeat this process until you feel calmer.

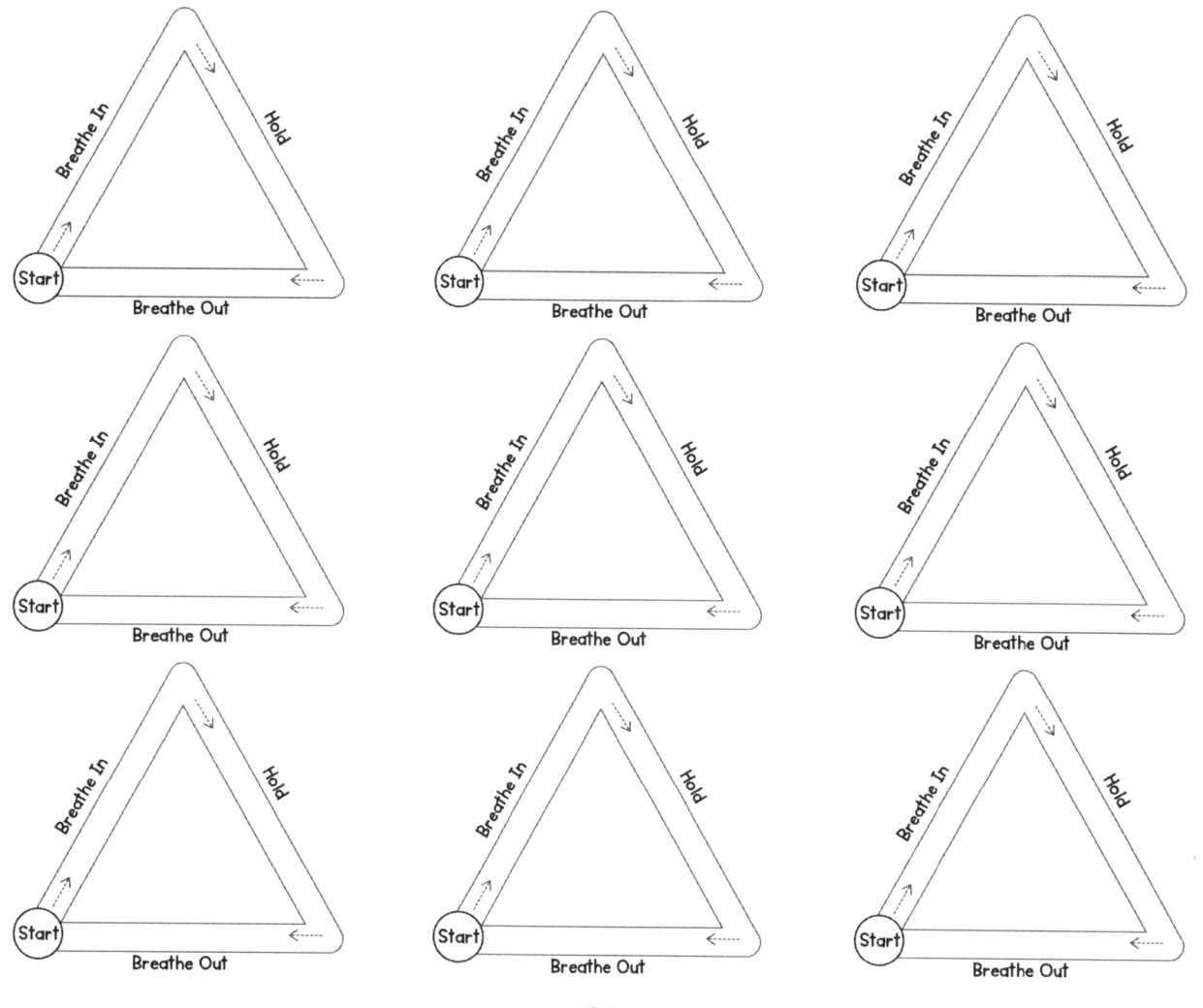

Triangle Breathing

Directions:

With any drawing tool, trace the outline of the shape. As you do, breathe in, hold your breath, and then breathe out. Repeat this process until you feel calmer.

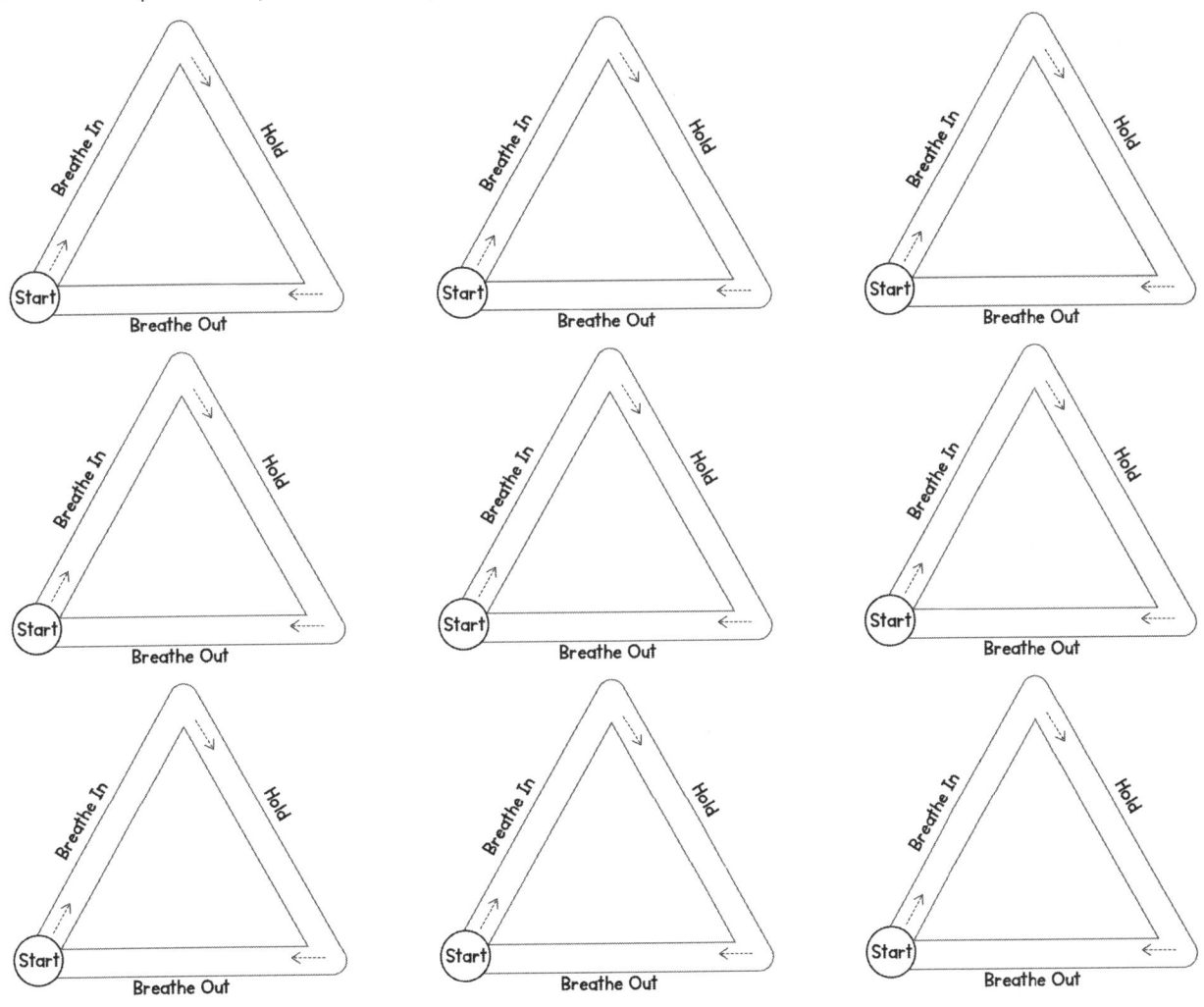

50

Box
Breathing

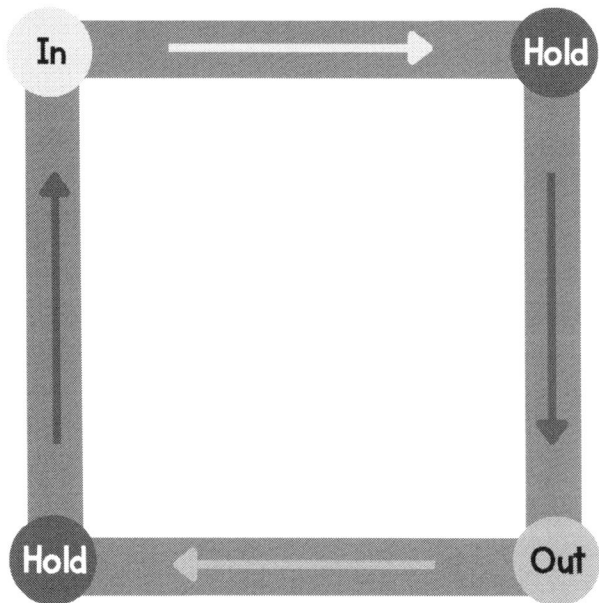

Box Breathing

Directions:

Use your finger to trace the outline of the shape, breathe in. Then trace your finger back as you breathe out. Do this at least 5 times or until you feel calmer.

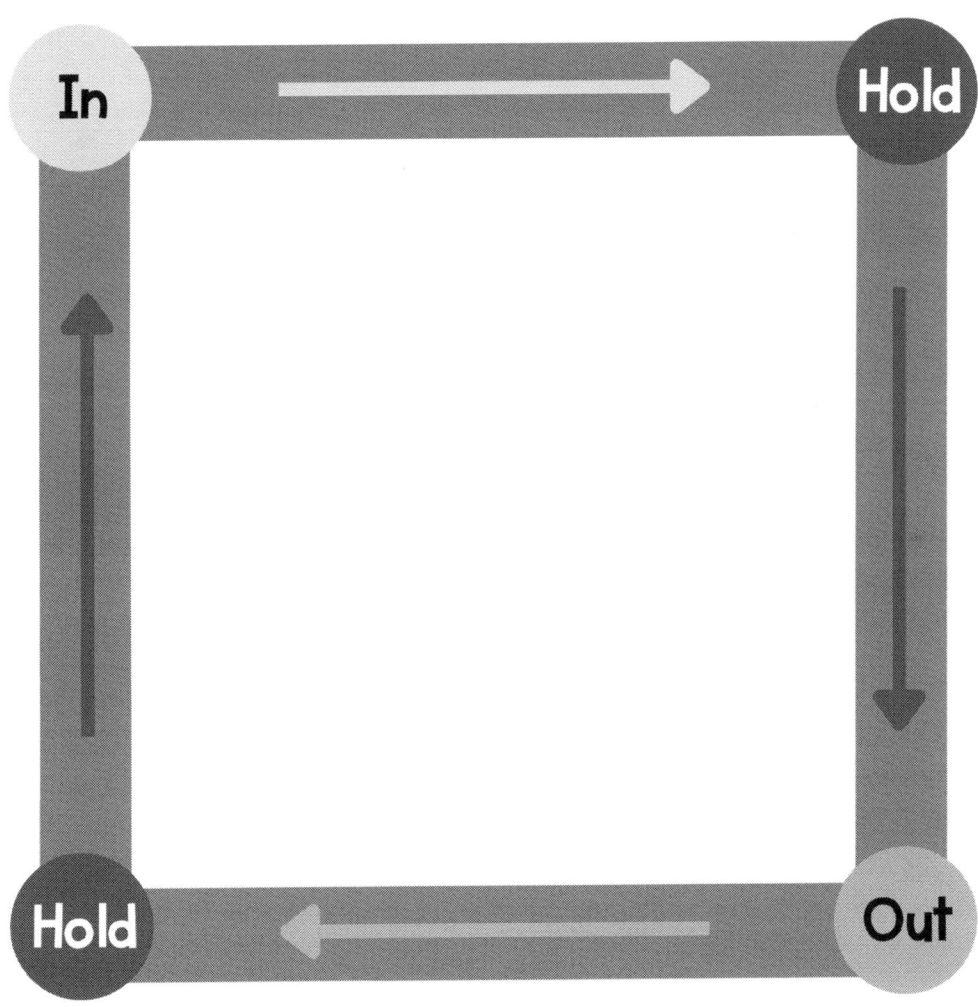

"Breathe and let be."

- Jon Kabat-Zinn

Box Breathing

Directions:

With any drawing tool, trace the outline of the shape. Breathe in, hold your breath, breathe out, then hold again. Repeat this process at least 5 times or until you feel calmer.

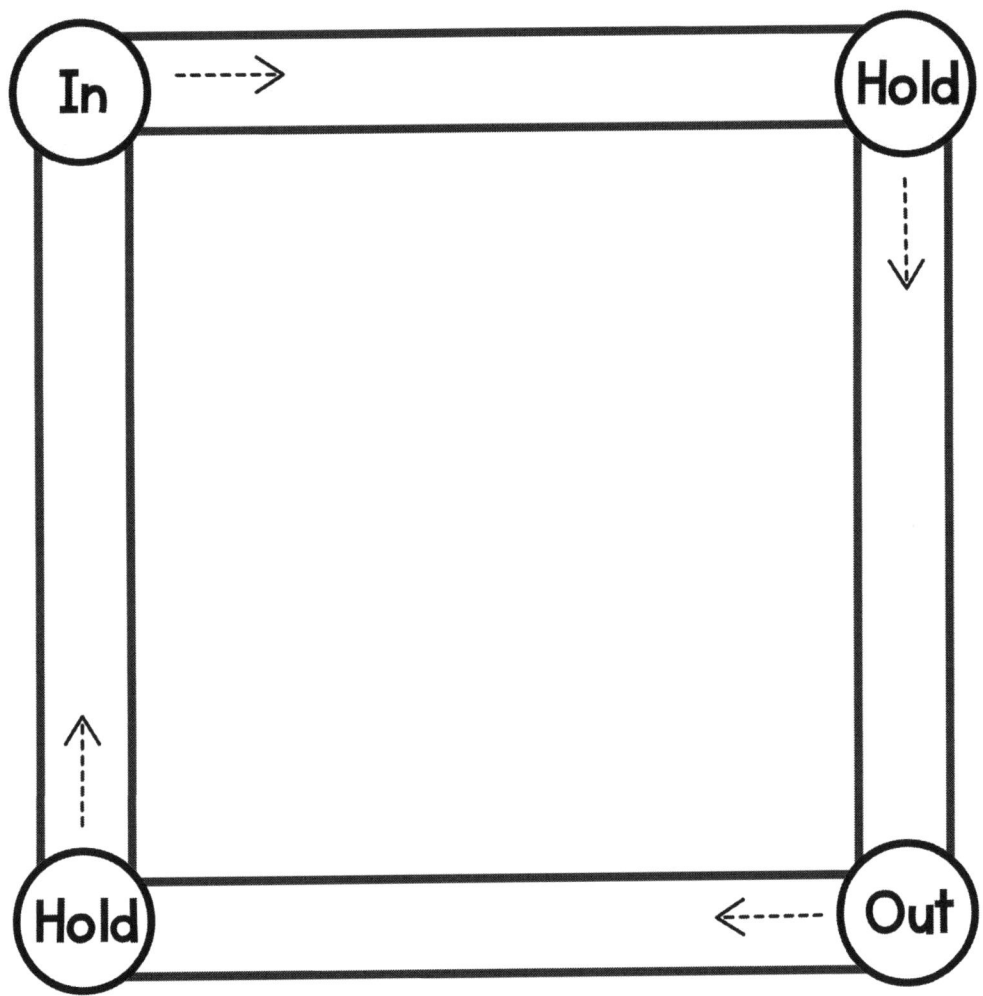

Box Breathing

Directions:

With any drawing tool, trace the outline of the shape. Breathe in, hold your breath, breathe out, then hold again. Repeat this process at least 5 times or until you feel calmer.

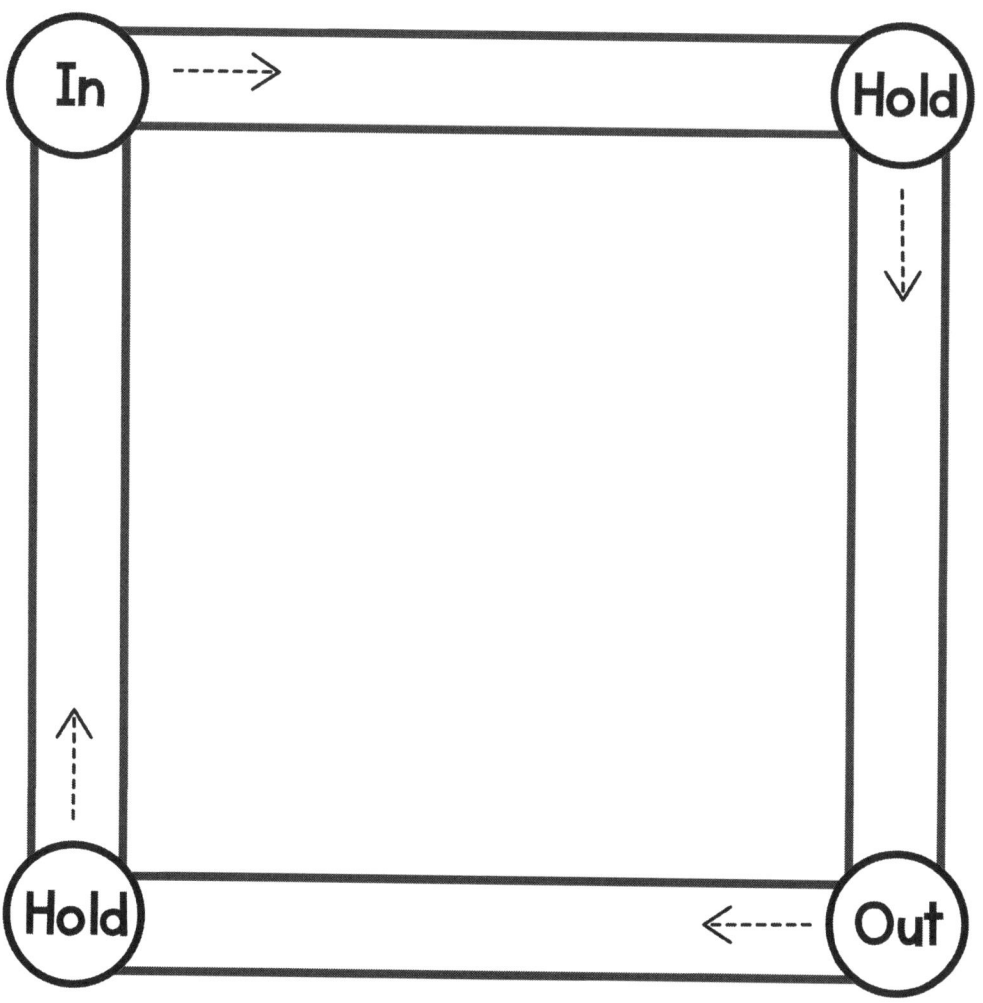

Box Breathing

Directions:

With any drawing tool, trace the outline of the shape. Breathe in, hold your breath, breathe out, then hold again. Repeat this process at least 5 times or until you feel calmer.

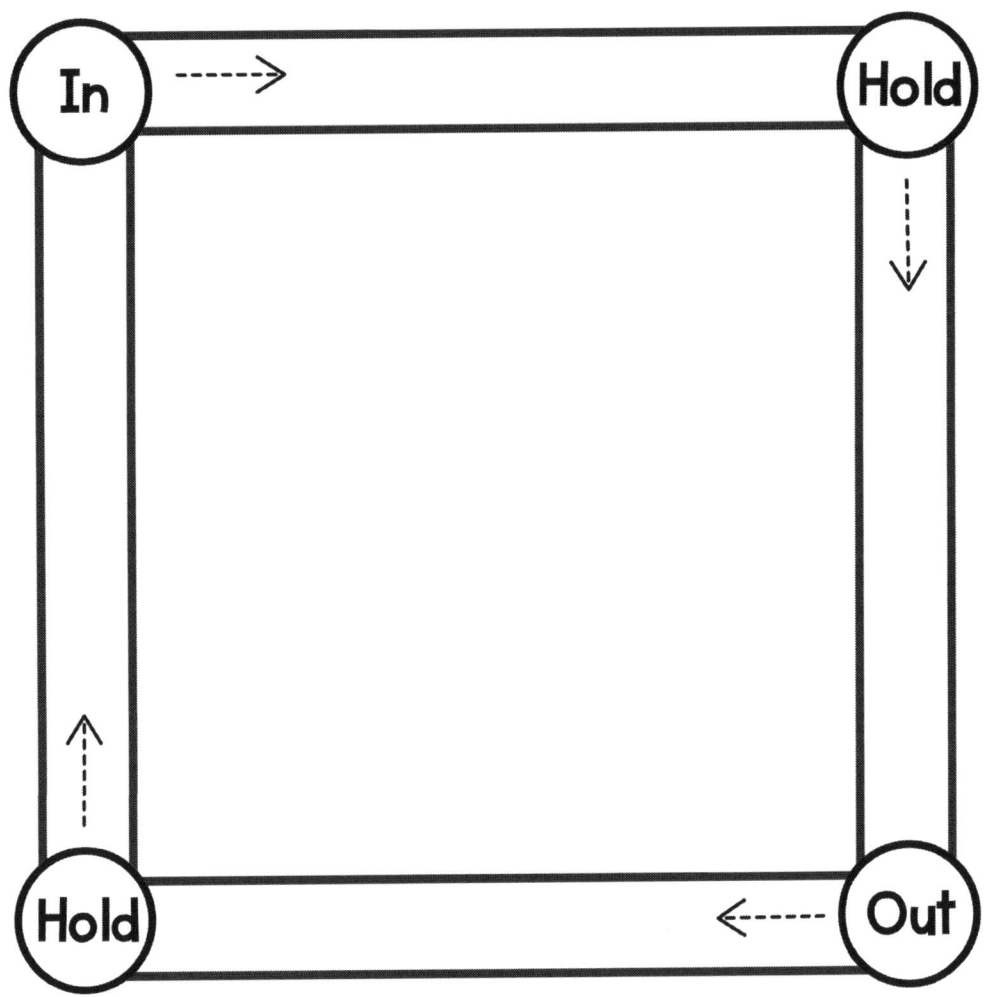

56

Box Breathing

Directions:

With any drawing tool, trace the outline of the shape. Breathe in, hold your breath, breathe out, then hold again. Repeat this process until you feel calmer.

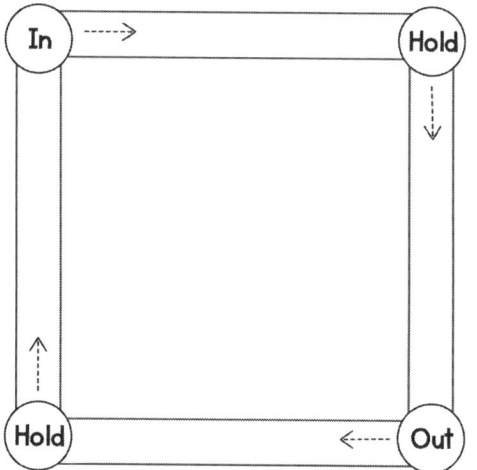

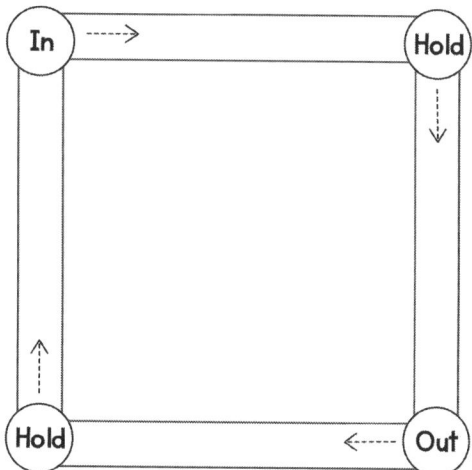

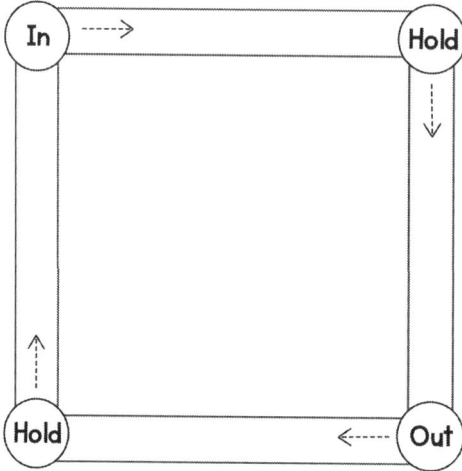

Box Breathing

Directions:

With any drawing tool, trace the outline of the shape. Breathe in, hold your breath, breathe out, then hold again. Repeat this process until you feel calmer.

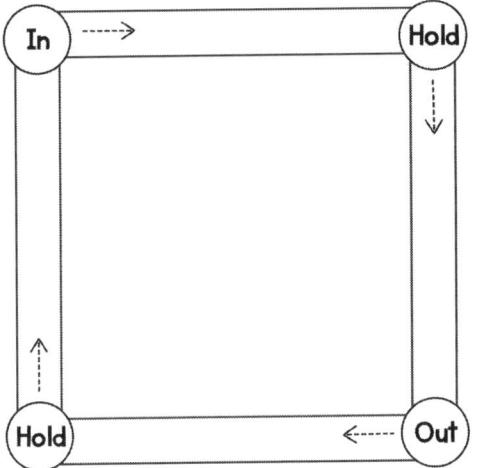

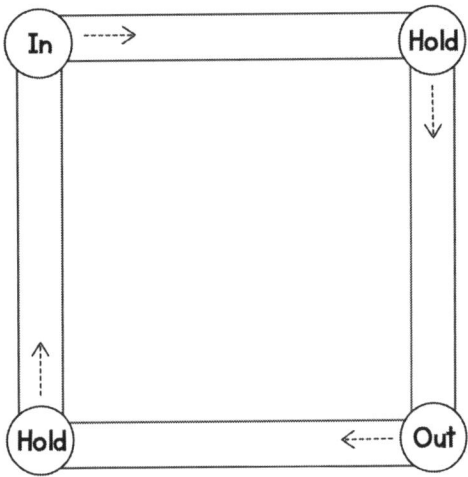

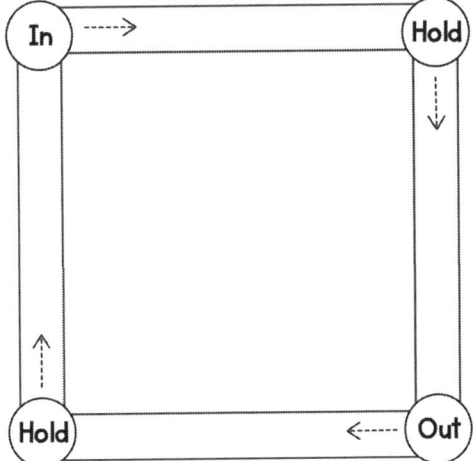

Box Breathing

Directions:

With any drawing tool, trace the outline of the shape. Breathe in, hold your breath, breathe out, then hold again. Repeat this process until you feel calmer.

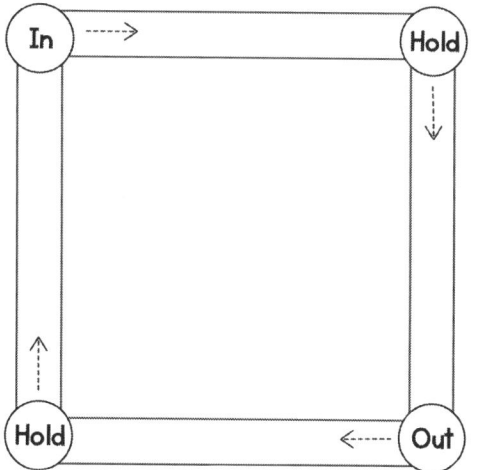

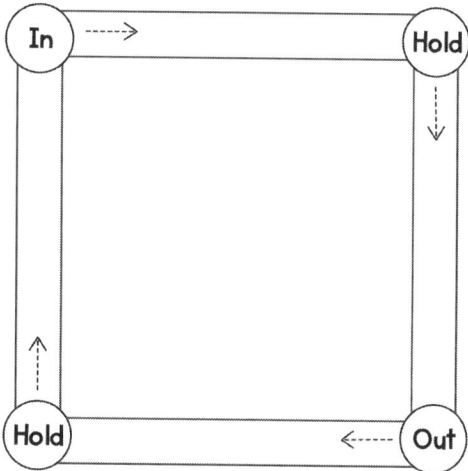

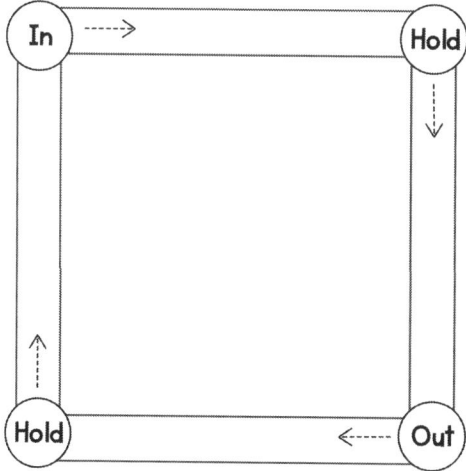

Box Breathing

Directions:

With any drawing tool, trace the outline of the shape. Breathe in, hold your breath, breathe out, then hold again. Repeat this process until you feel calmer.

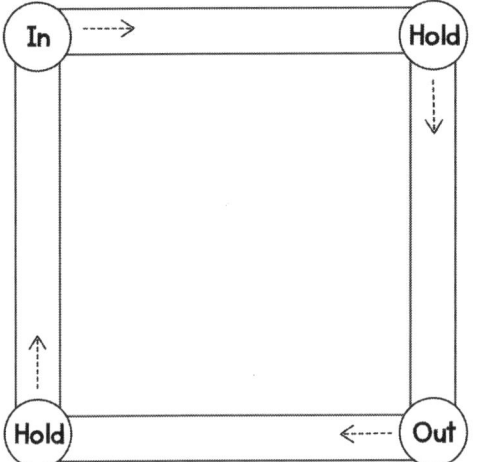

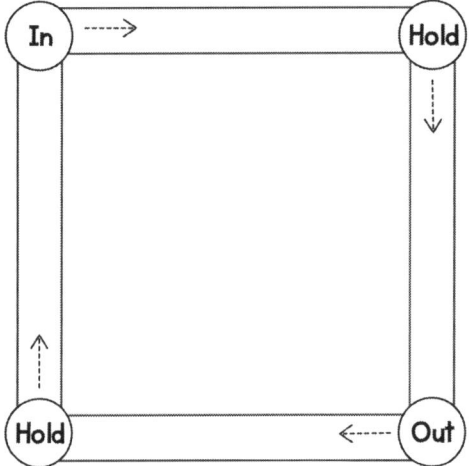

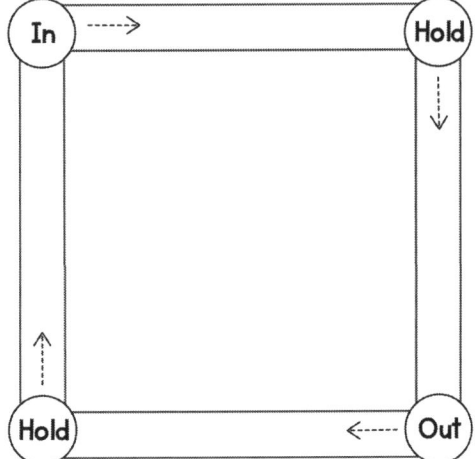

60

Box Breathing

Directions:

With any drawing tool, trace the outline of the shape. Breathe in, hold your breath, breathe out, then hold again. Repeat this process until you feel calmer.

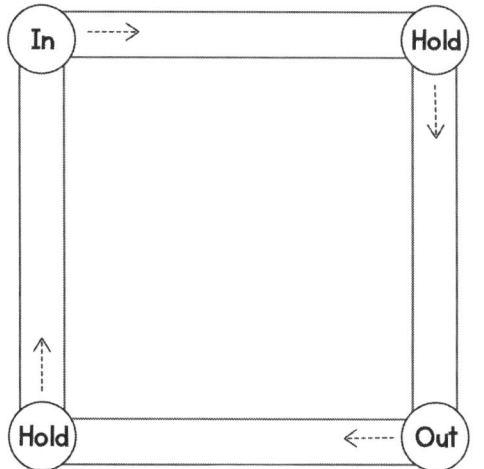

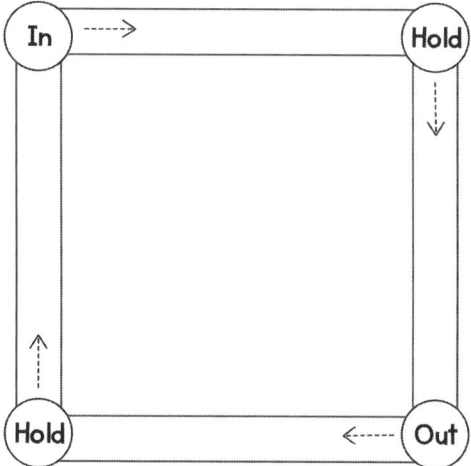

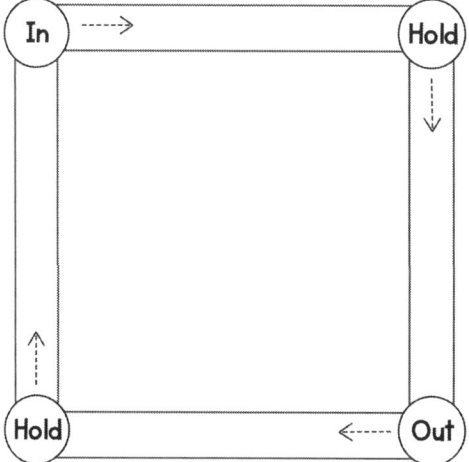

Box Breathing

Directions:

With any drawing tool, trace the outline of the shape. Breathe in, hold your breath, breathe out, then hold again. Repeat this process until you feel calmer.

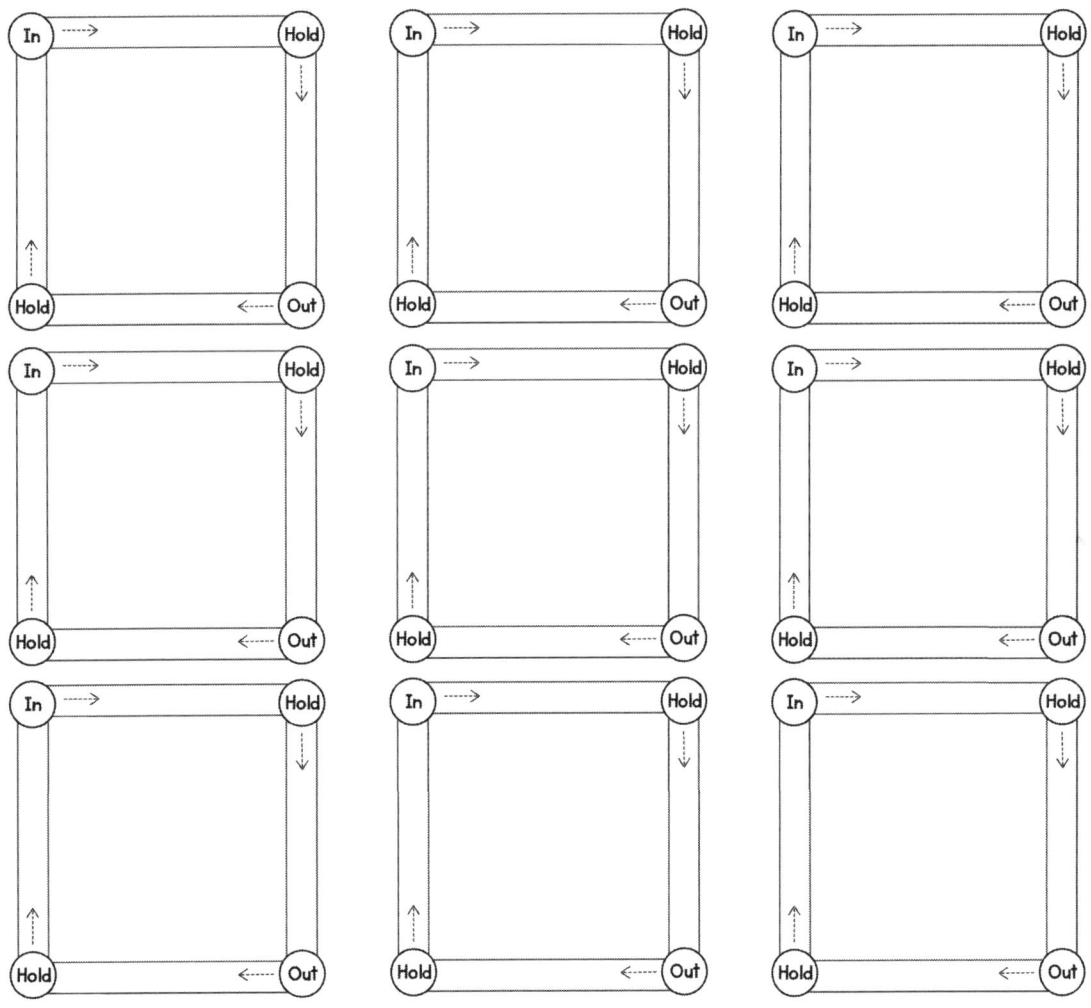

62

Box Breathing

Directions:

With any drawing tool, trace the outline of the shape. Breathe in, hold your breath, breathe out, then hold again. Repeat this process until you feel calmer.

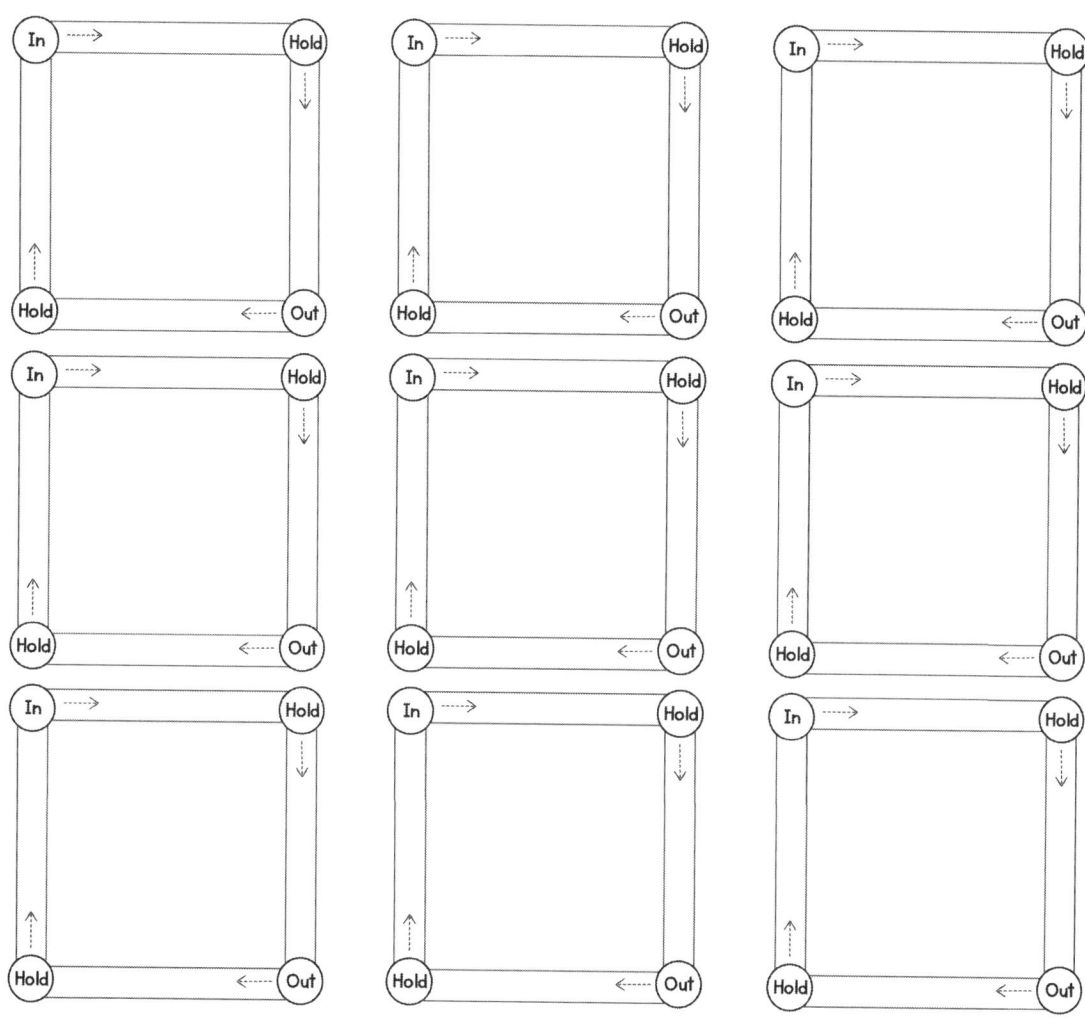

Box Breathing

Directions:

With any drawing tool, trace the outline of the shape. Breathe in, hold your breath, breathe out, then hold again. Repeat this process until you feel calmer.

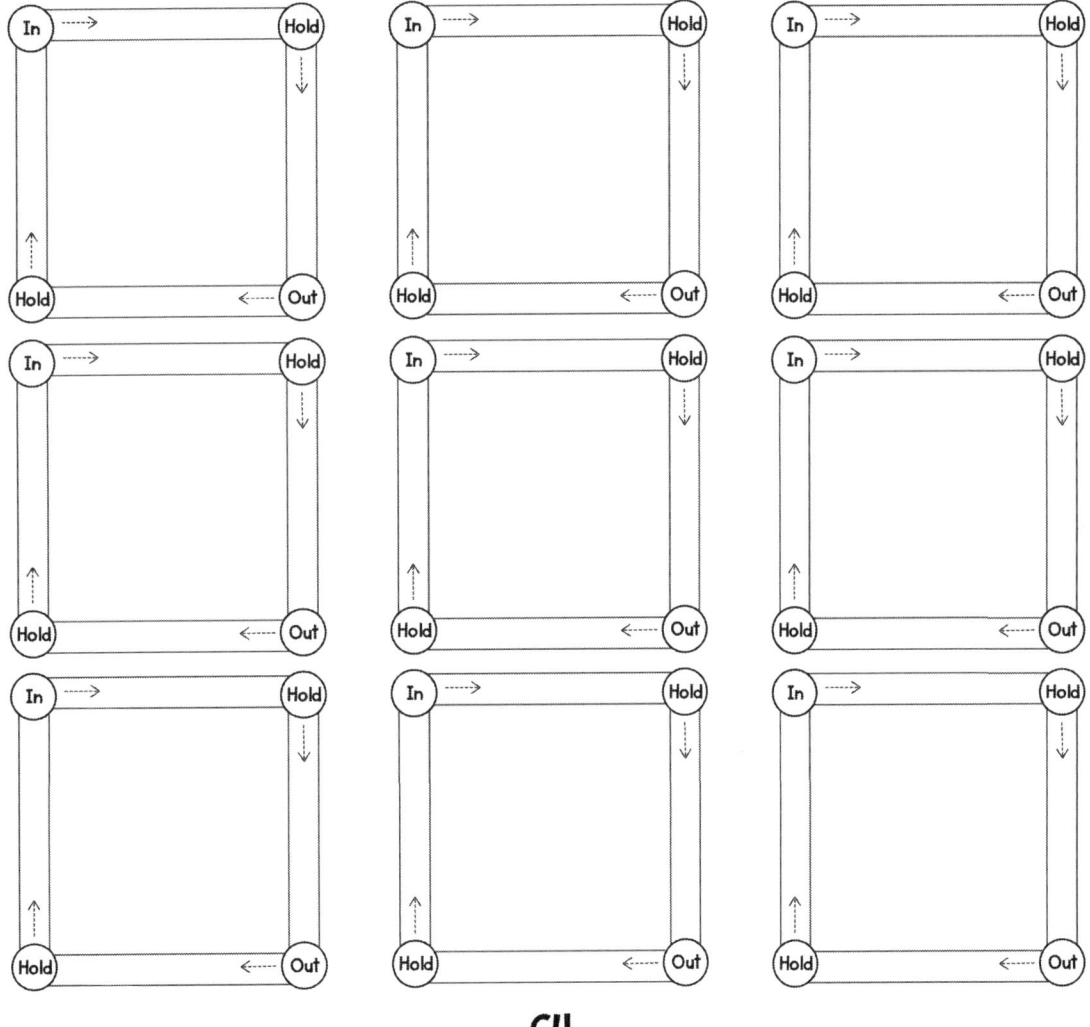

64

Box Breathing

Directions:

With any drawing tool, trace the outline of the shape. Breathe in, hold your breath, breathe out, then hold again. Repeat this process until you feel calmer.

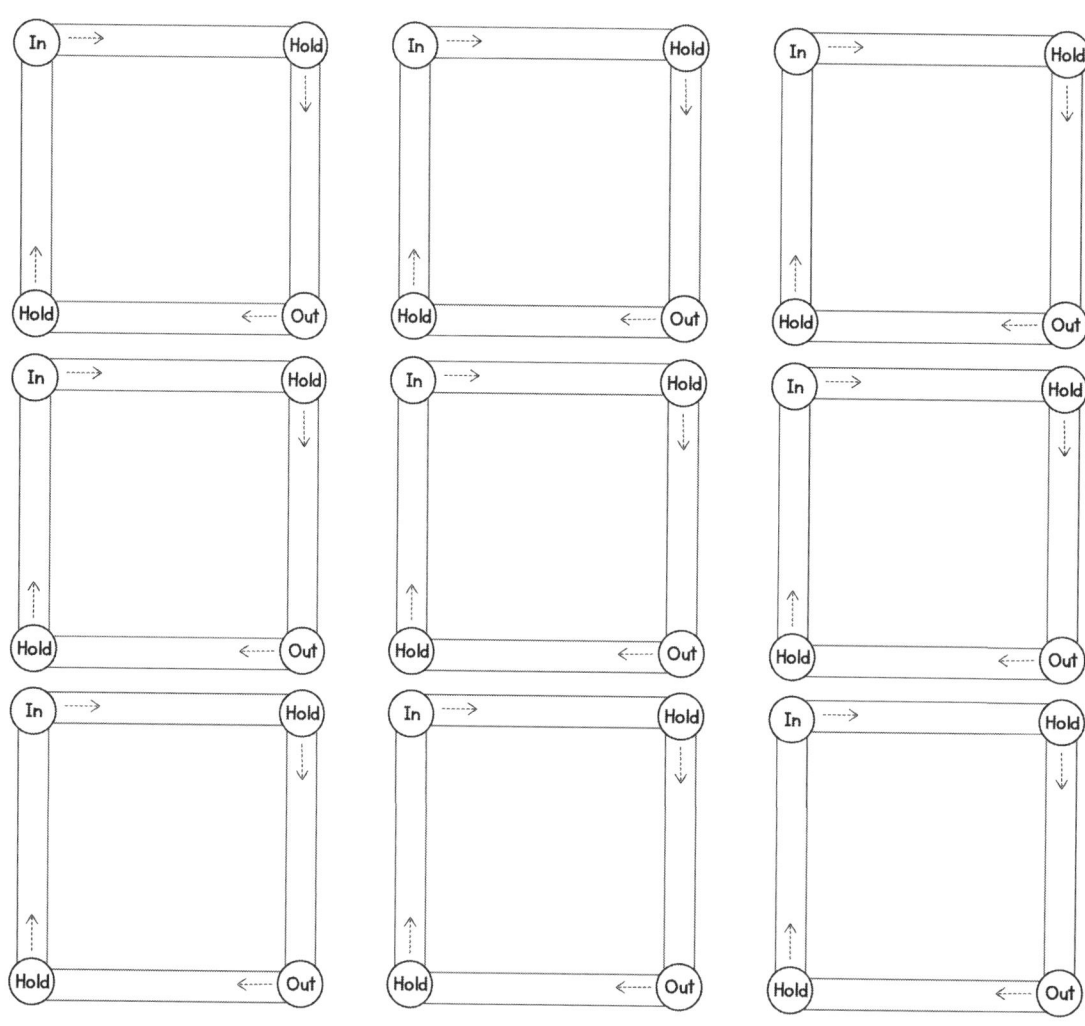

Box Breathing

With any drawing tool, trace the outline of the shape. Breathe in, hold your breath, breathe out, then hold again. Repeat this process until you feel calmer.

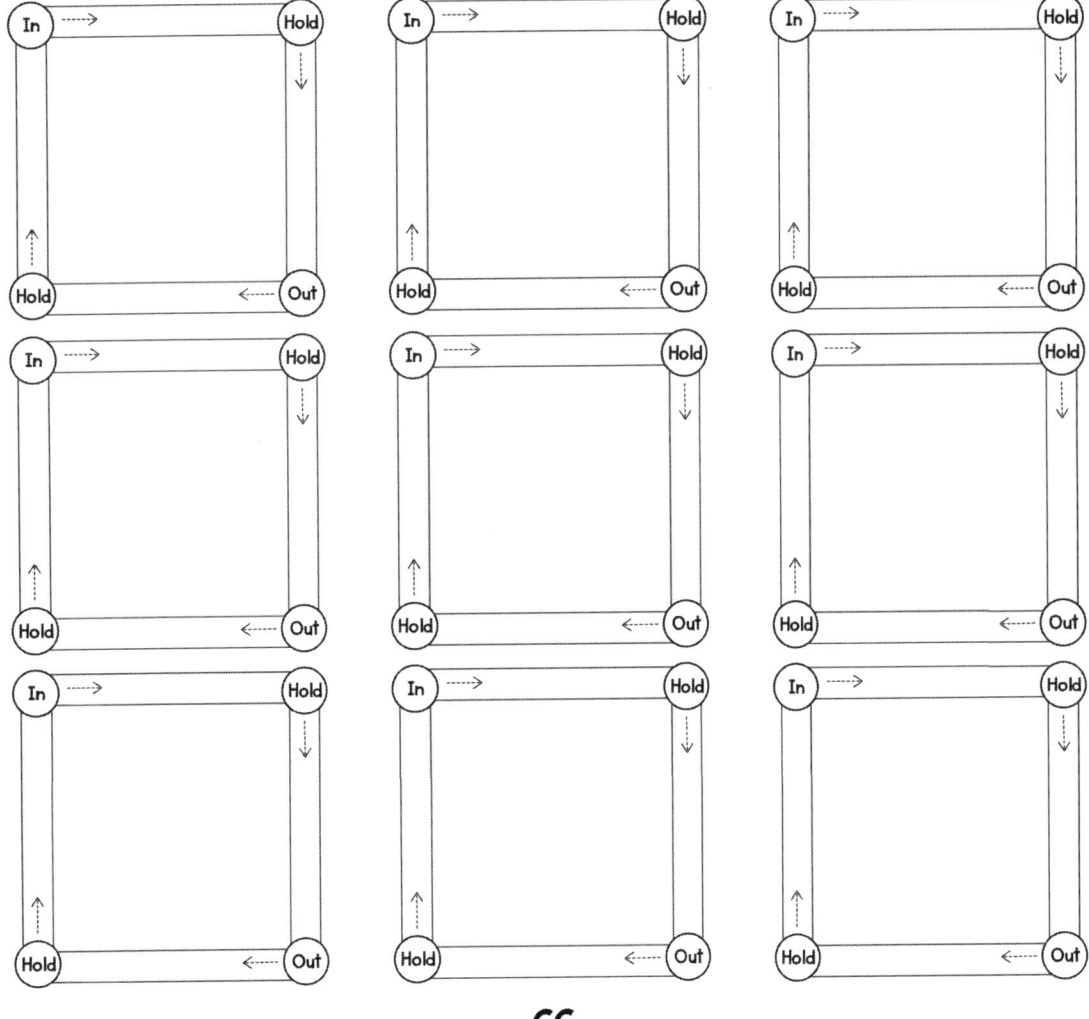

66

Lazy 8 Breathing

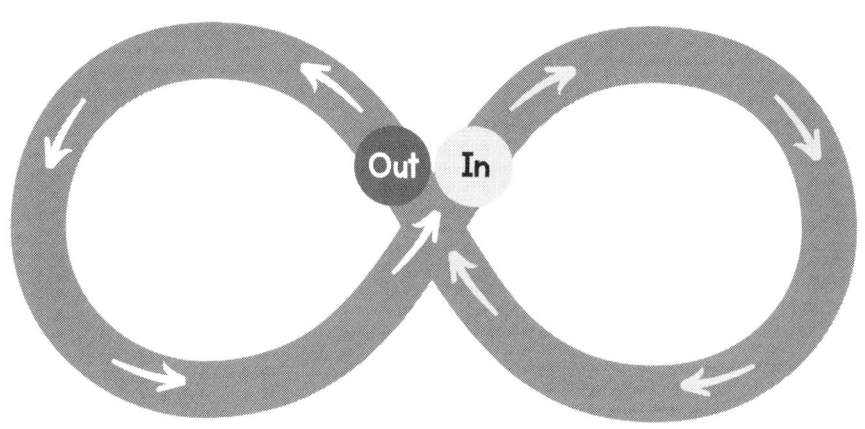

Lazy 8 Breathing

Directions:

Use your finger to trace the outline of the shape, breathe in and out as you go. Do this for at least 5 times or until you feel calmer.

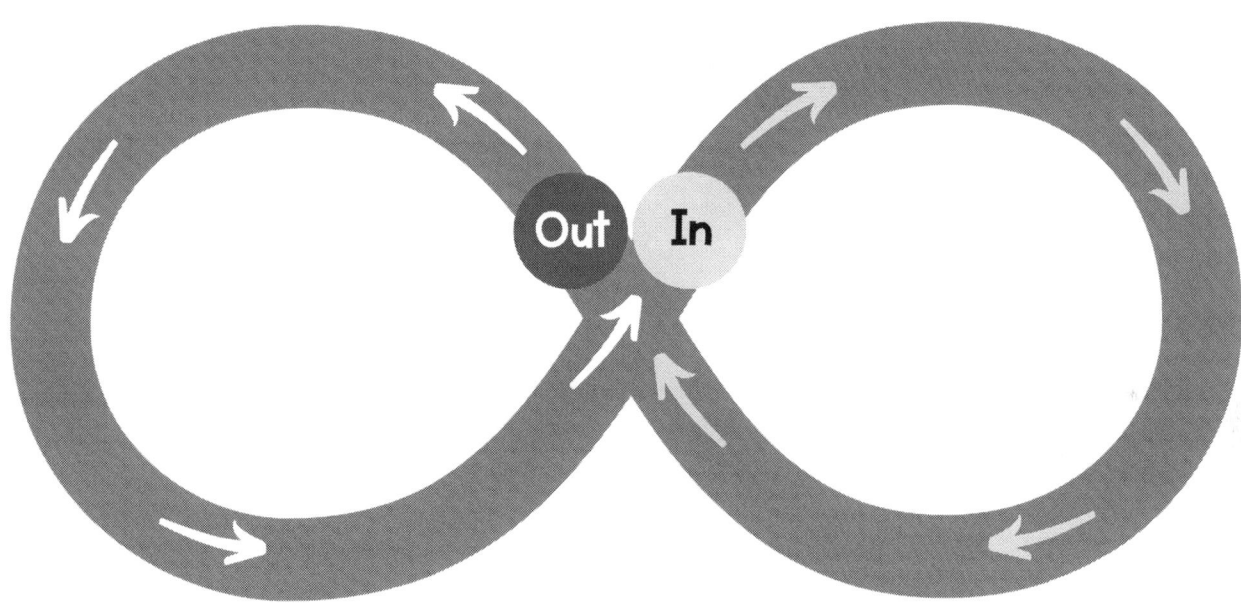

"Believe you can, then you will."

- Mulan

Lazy 8 Breathing

With any drawing tool, trace the outline of the shape, breathing in and out as you go. Repeat this process at least 5 times or until you feel calmer.

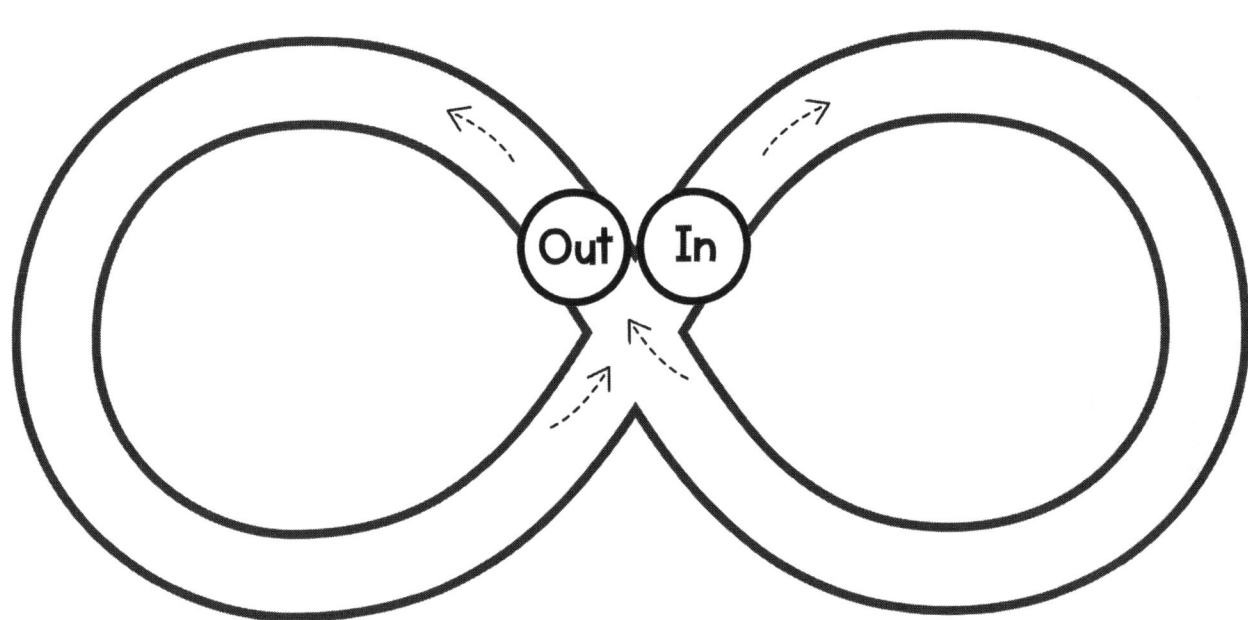

70

Lazy 8 Breathing

<u>Directions:</u>

With any drawing tool, trace the outline of the shape, breathing in and out as you go. Repeat this process at least 5 times or until you feel calmer.

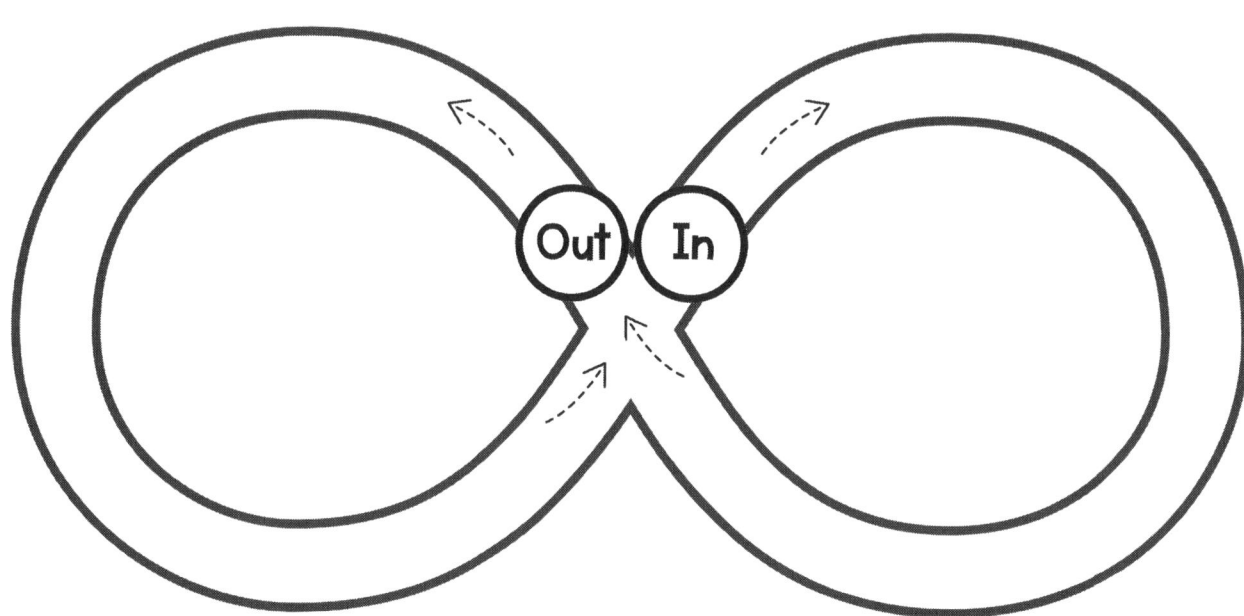

Lazy 8 Breathing

Directions:

With any drawing tool, trace the outline of the shape, breathing in and out as you go. Repeat this process at least 5 times or until you feel calmer.

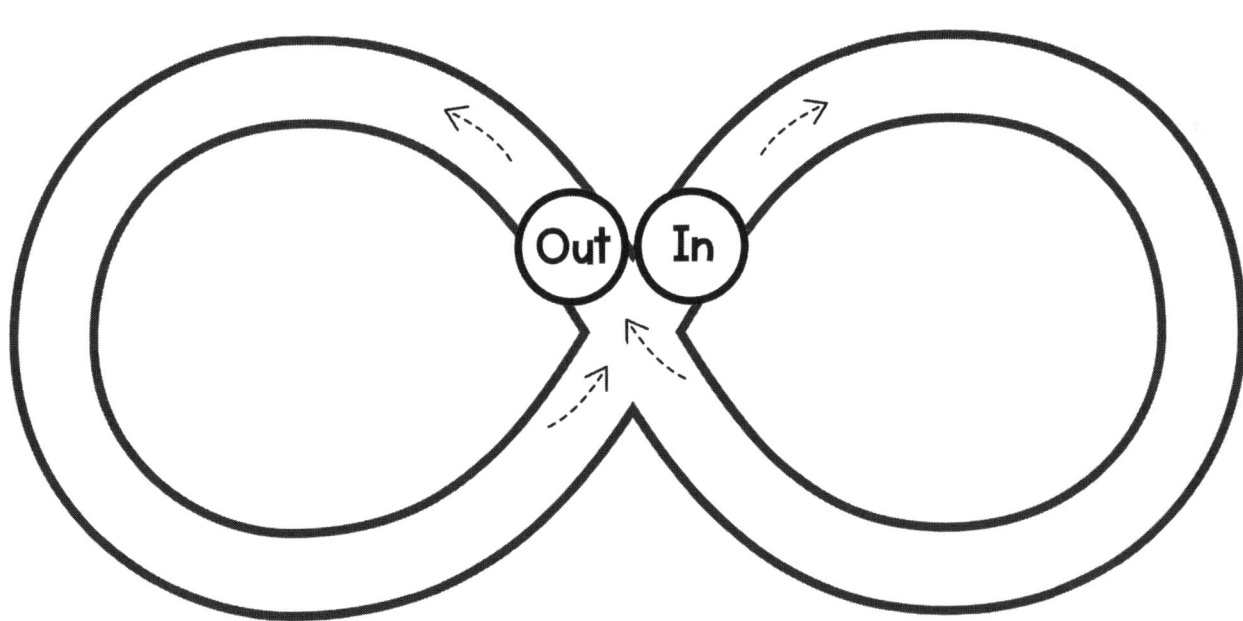

72

Lazy 8 Breathing

Directions:

With any drawing tool, trace the outline of the shape, breathing in and out as you go. Repeat this process until you feel calmer.

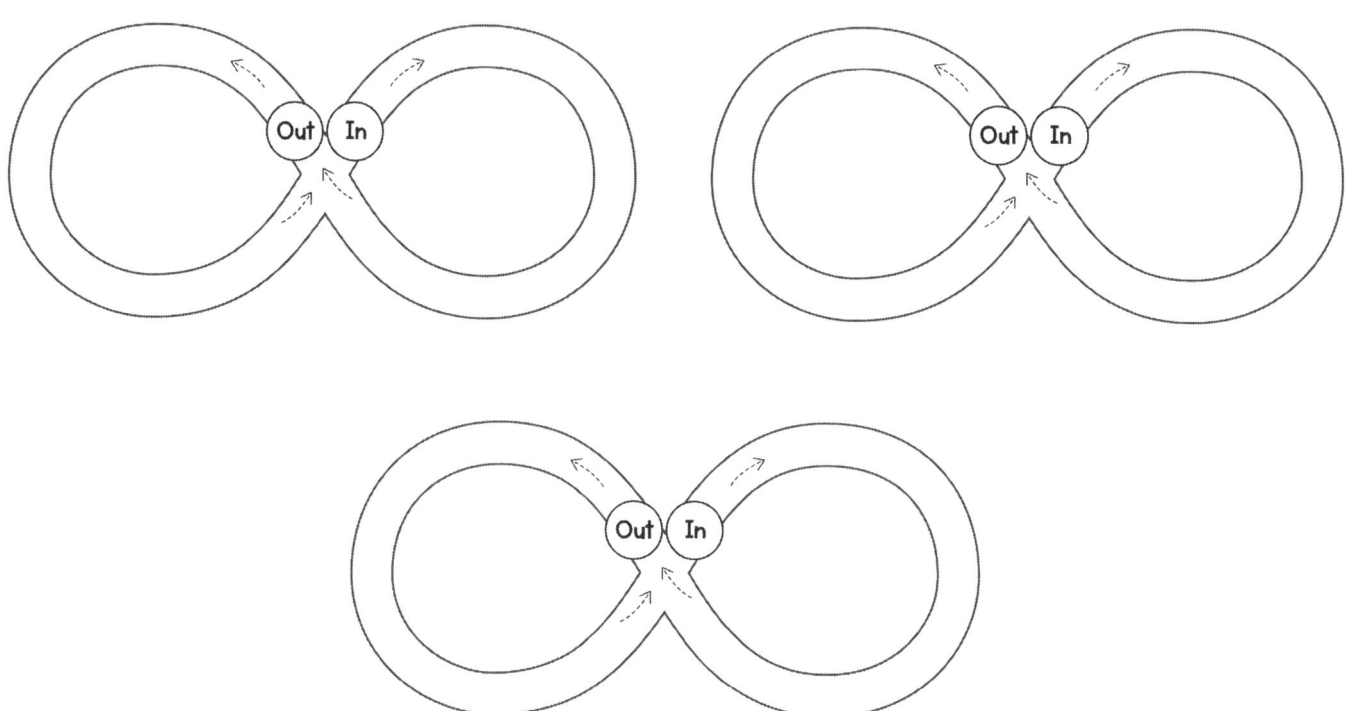

Lazy 8 Breathing

Directions:

With any drawing tool, trace the outline of the shape, breathing in and out as you go. Repeat this process until you feel calmer.

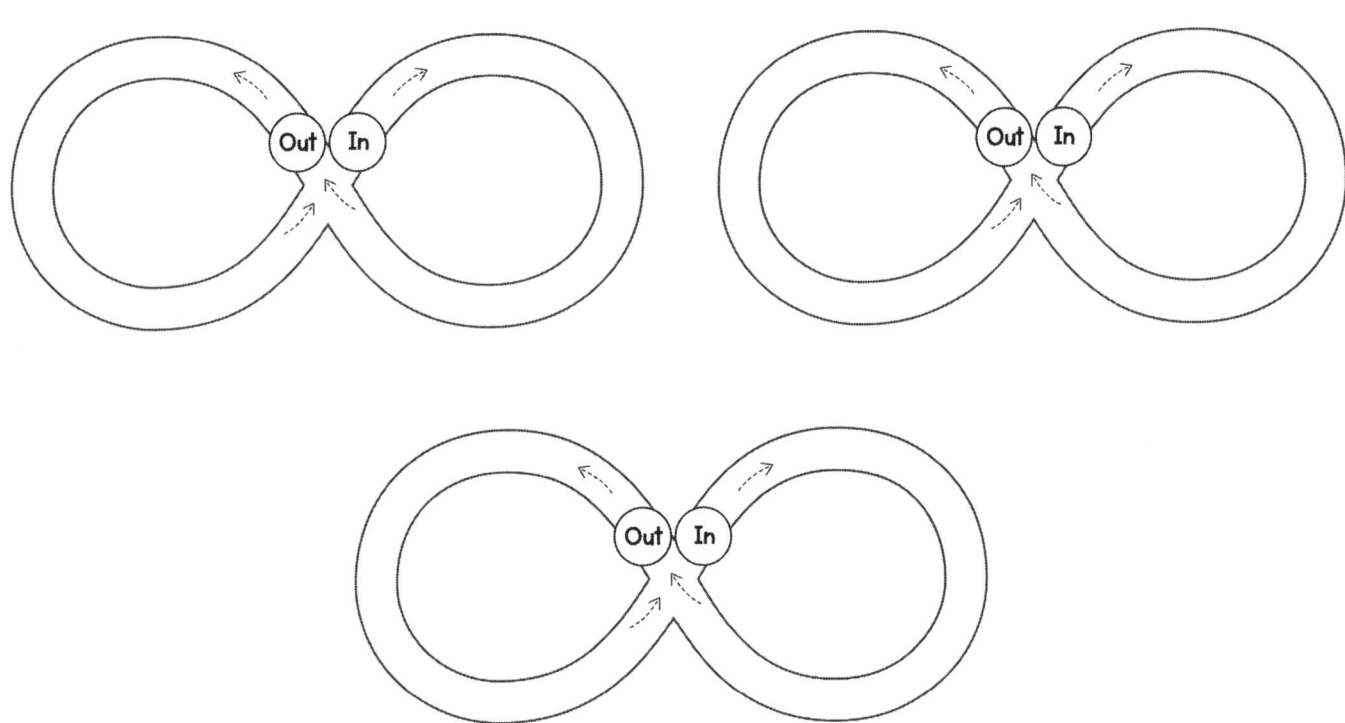

Lazy 8 Breathing

Directions:

With any drawing tool, trace the outline of the shape, breathing in and out as you go. Repeat this process until you feel calmer.

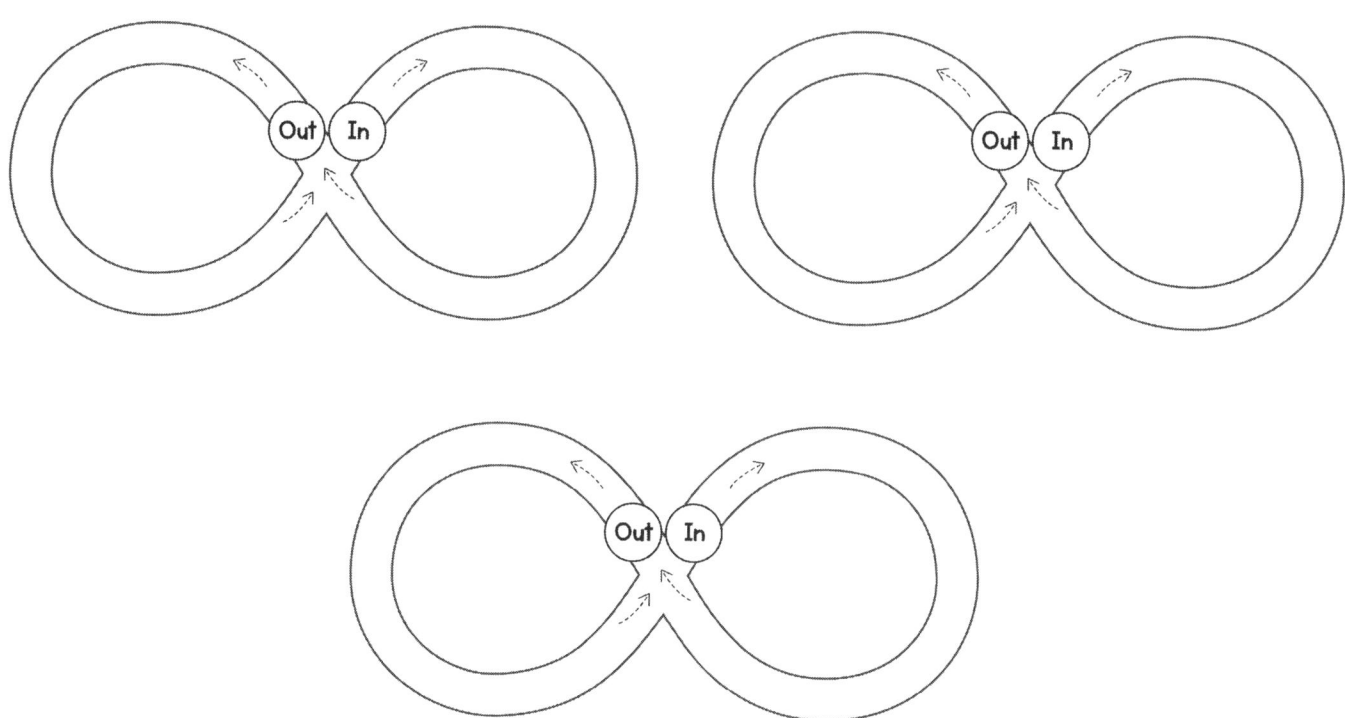

Lazy 8 Breathing

Directions:

With any drawing tool, trace the outline of the shape, breathing in and out as you go. Repeat this process until you feel calmer.

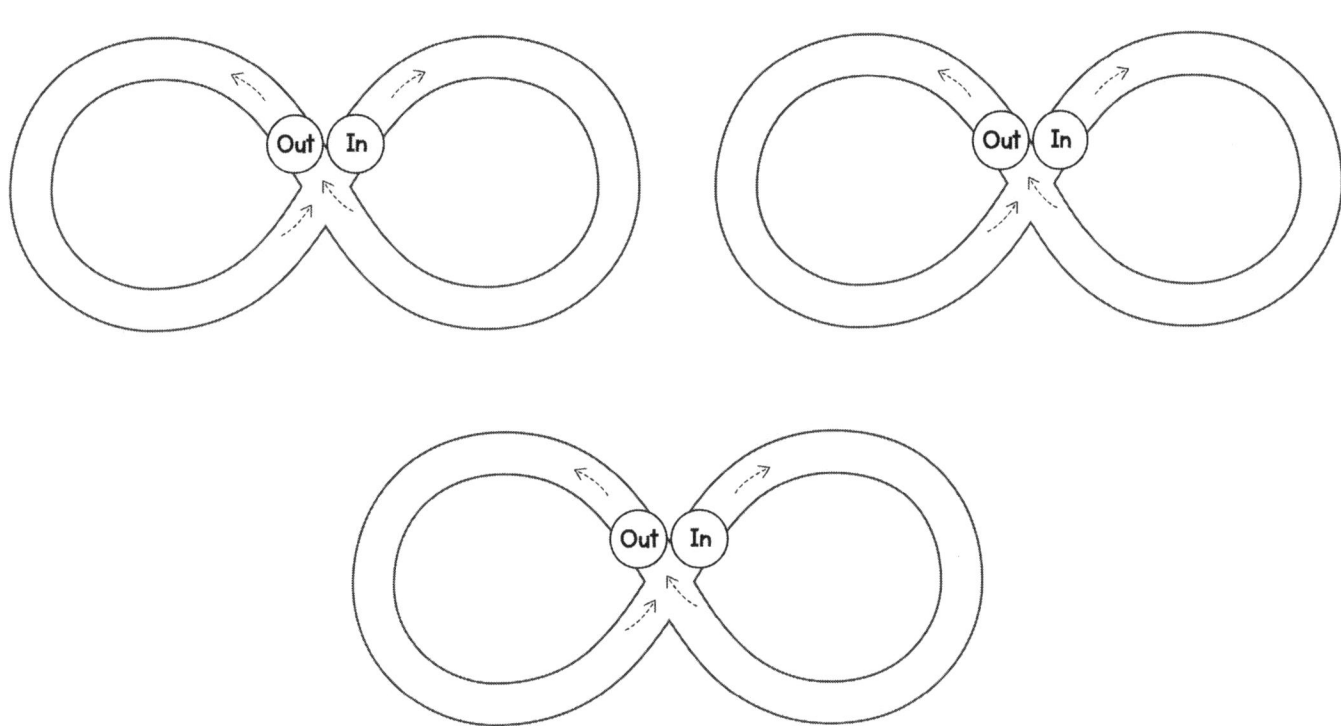

Lazy 8 Breathing

<u>Directions:</u>

With any drawing tool, trace the outline of the shape, breathing in and out as you go. Repeat this process until you feel calmer.

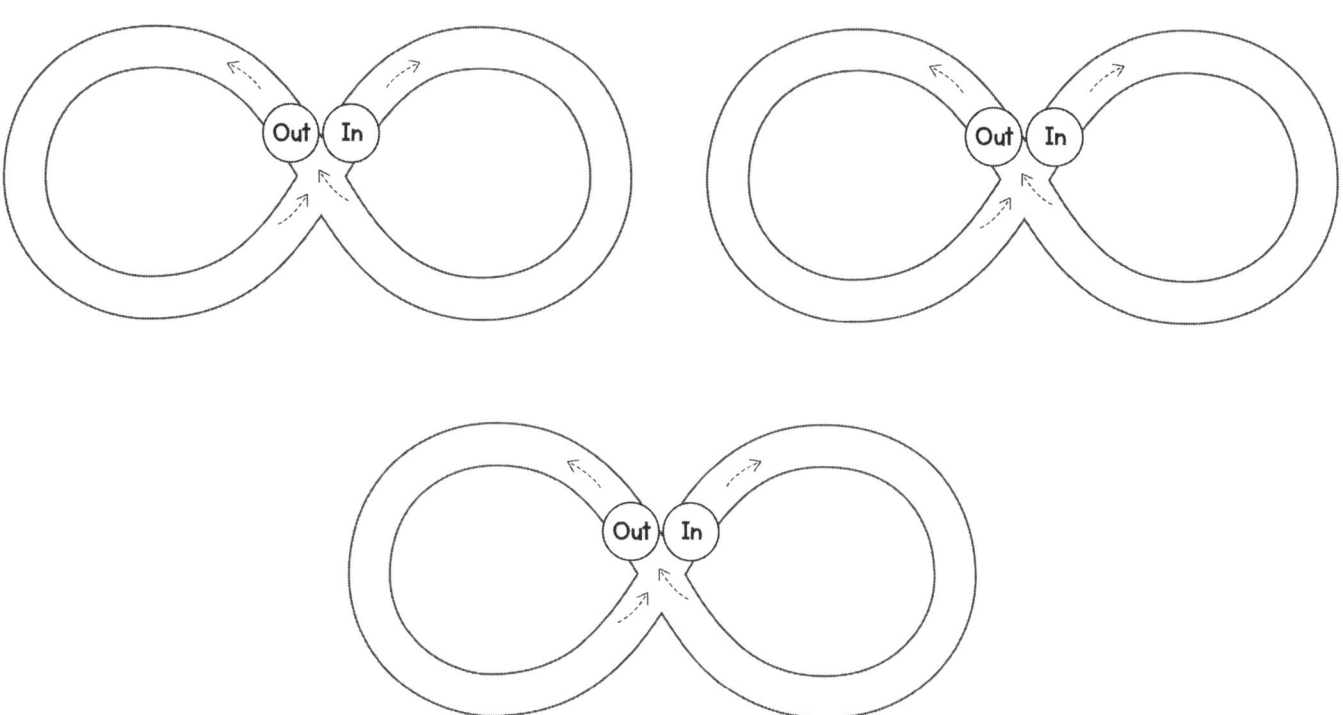

Lazy 8 Breathing

Directions:

With any drawing tool, trace the outline of the shape, breathing in and out as you go. Repeat this process until you feel calmer.

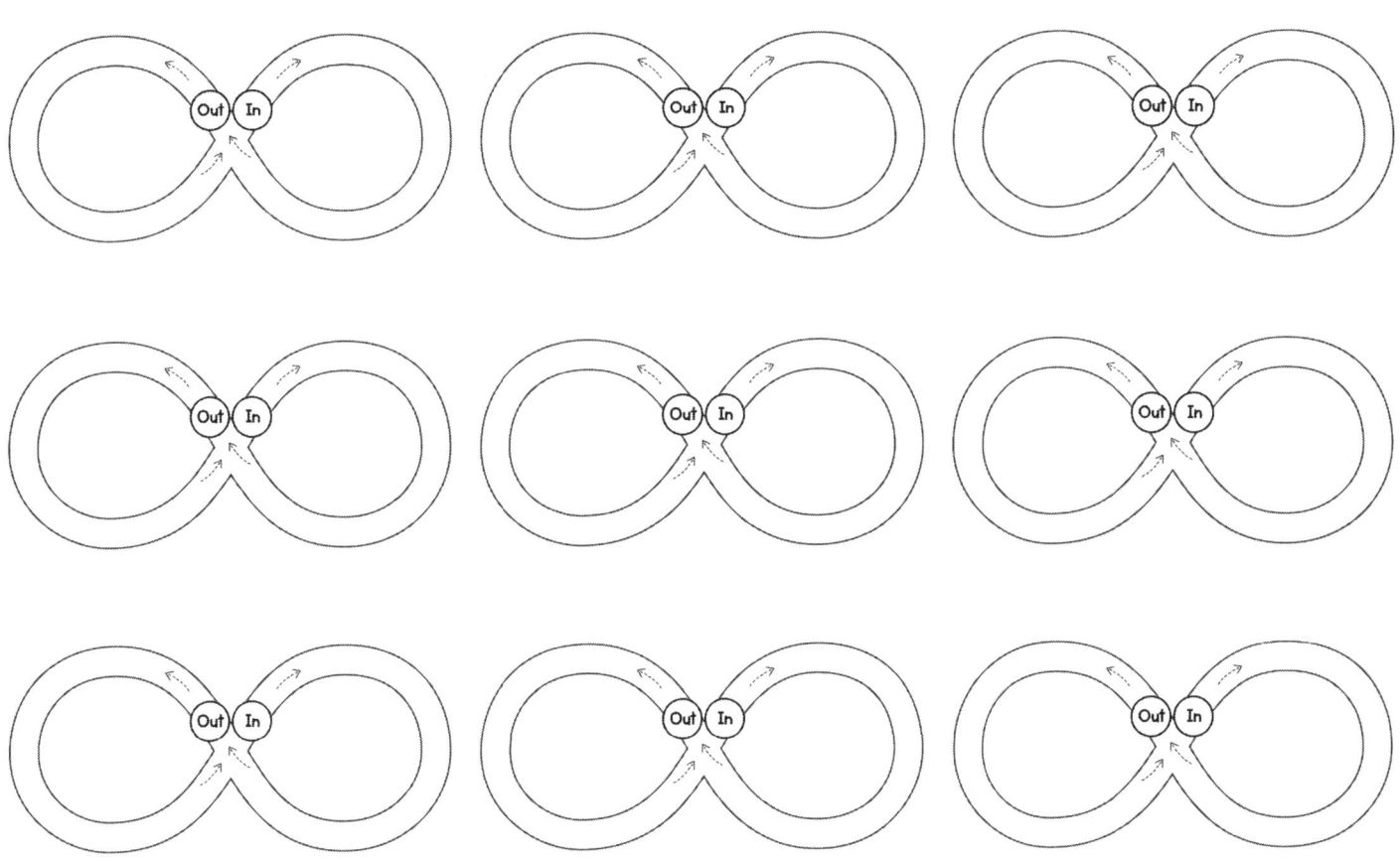

Lazy 8 Breathing

Directions:

With any drawing tool, trace the outline of the shape, breathing in and out as you go. Repeat this process until you feel calmer.

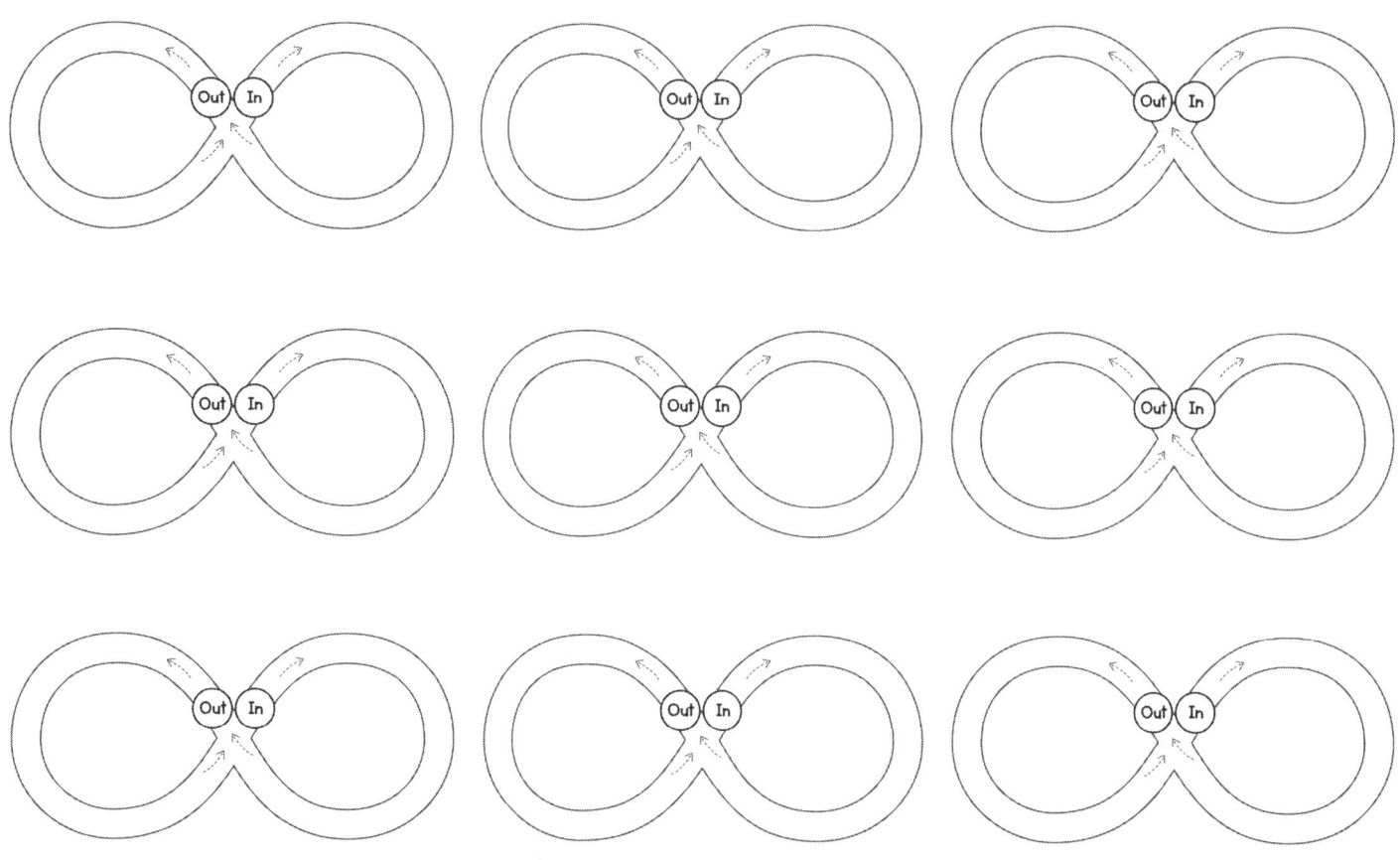

Lazy 8 Breathing

Directions:

With any drawing tool, trace the outline of the shape, breathing in and out as you go. Repeat this process until you feel calmer.

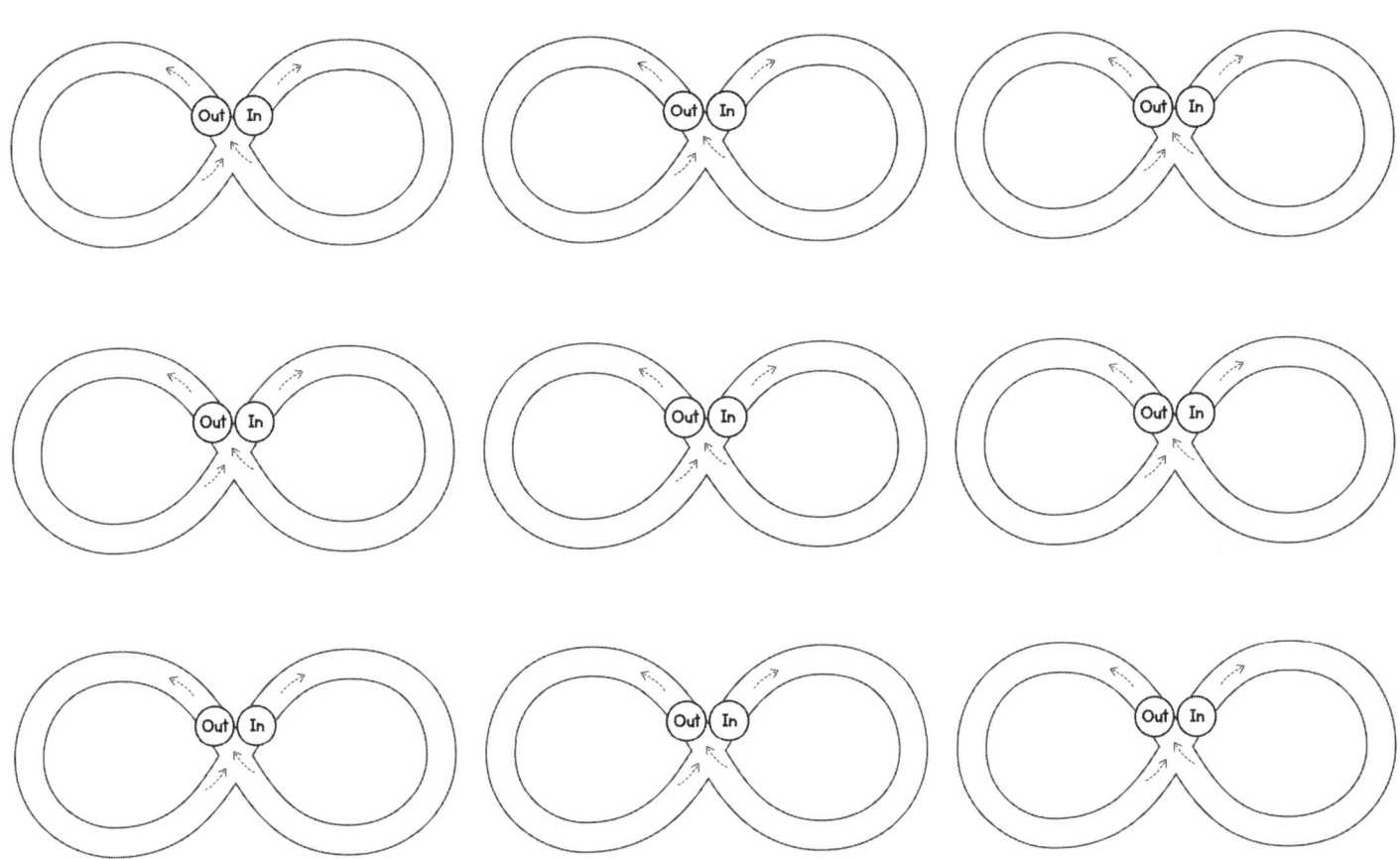

Lazy 8 Breathing

<u>Directions:</u>

With any drawing tool, trace the outline of the shape, breathing in and out as you go. Repeat this process until you feel calmer.

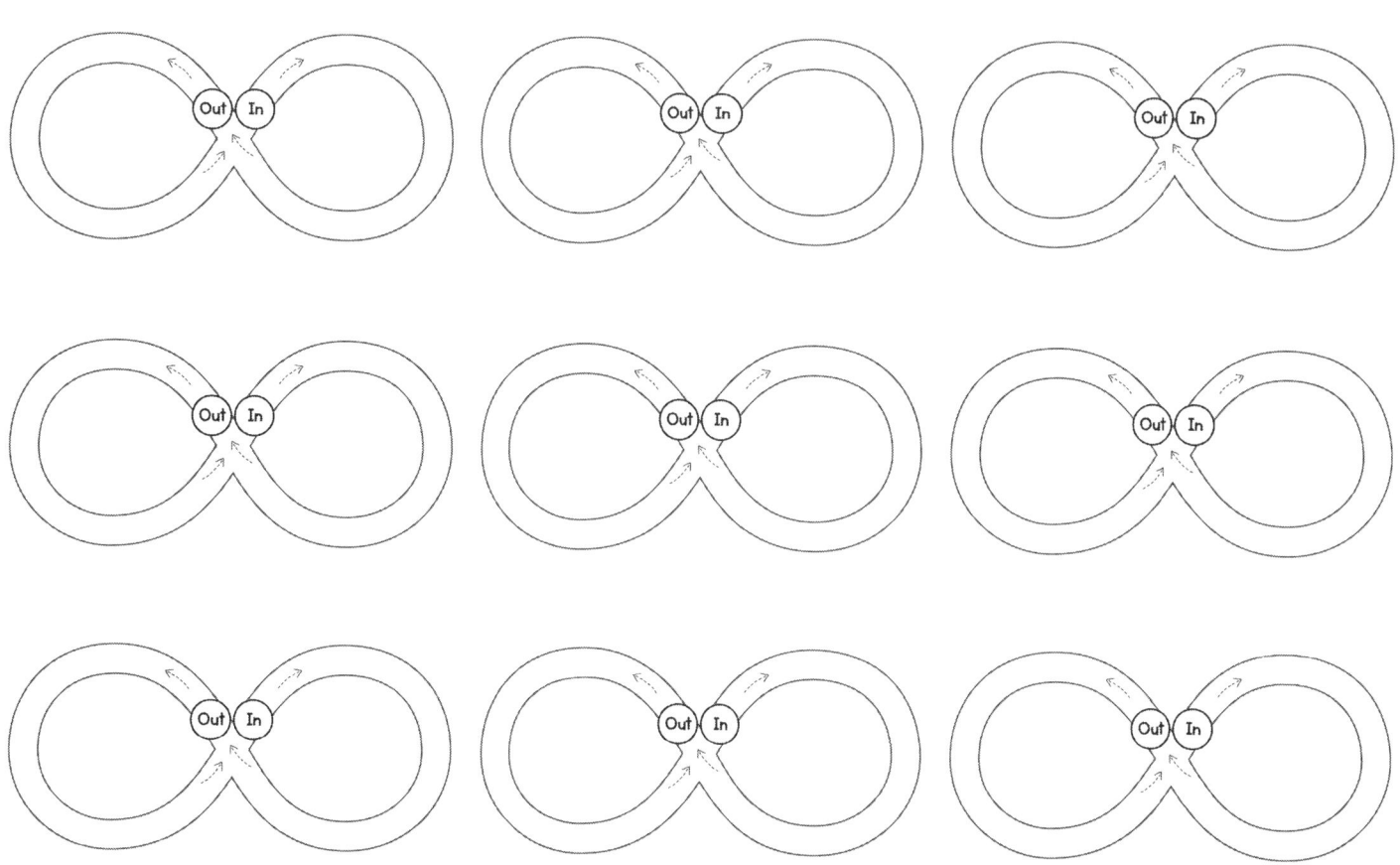

Lazy 8 Breathing

Directions:

With any drawing tool, trace the outline of the shape, breathing in and out as you go. Repeat this process until you feel calmer.

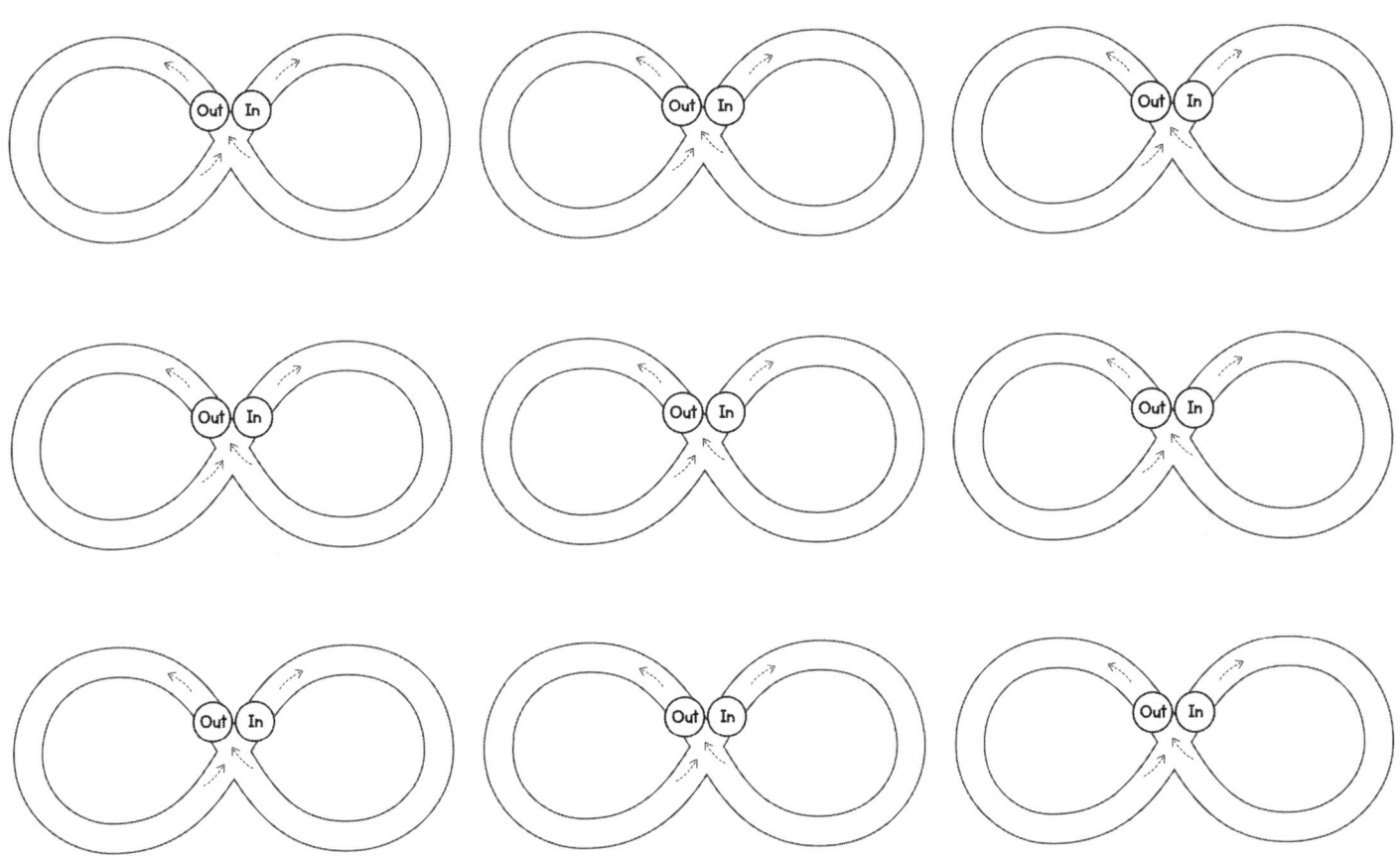

Lazy 8 Breathing

Directions:

With any drawing tool, trace the outline of the shape, breathing in and out as you go. Repeat this process until you feel calmer.

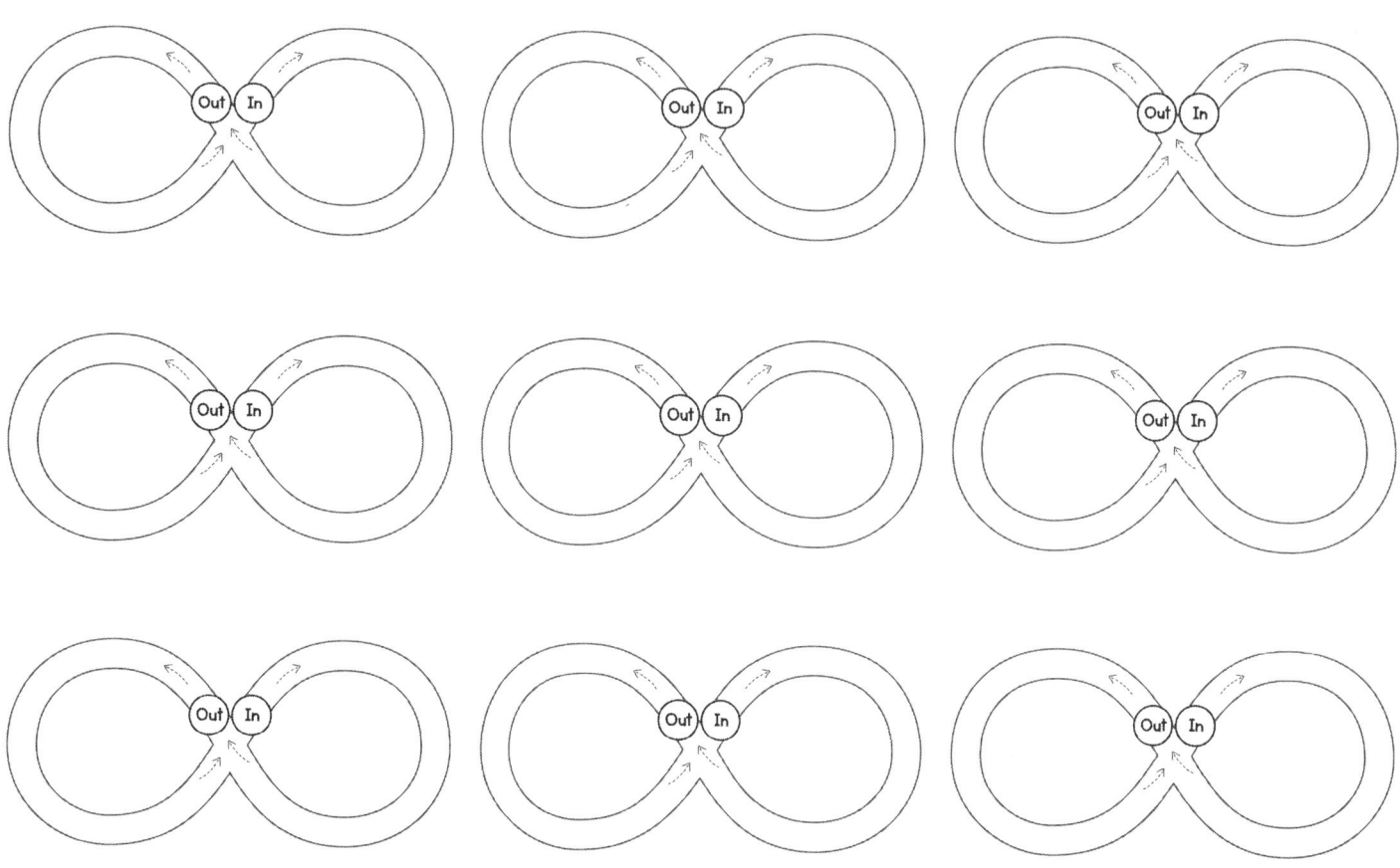

Lazy 8 Breathing

Directions:

With any drawing tool, trace the outline of the shape, breathing in and out as you go. Repeat this process until you feel calmer.

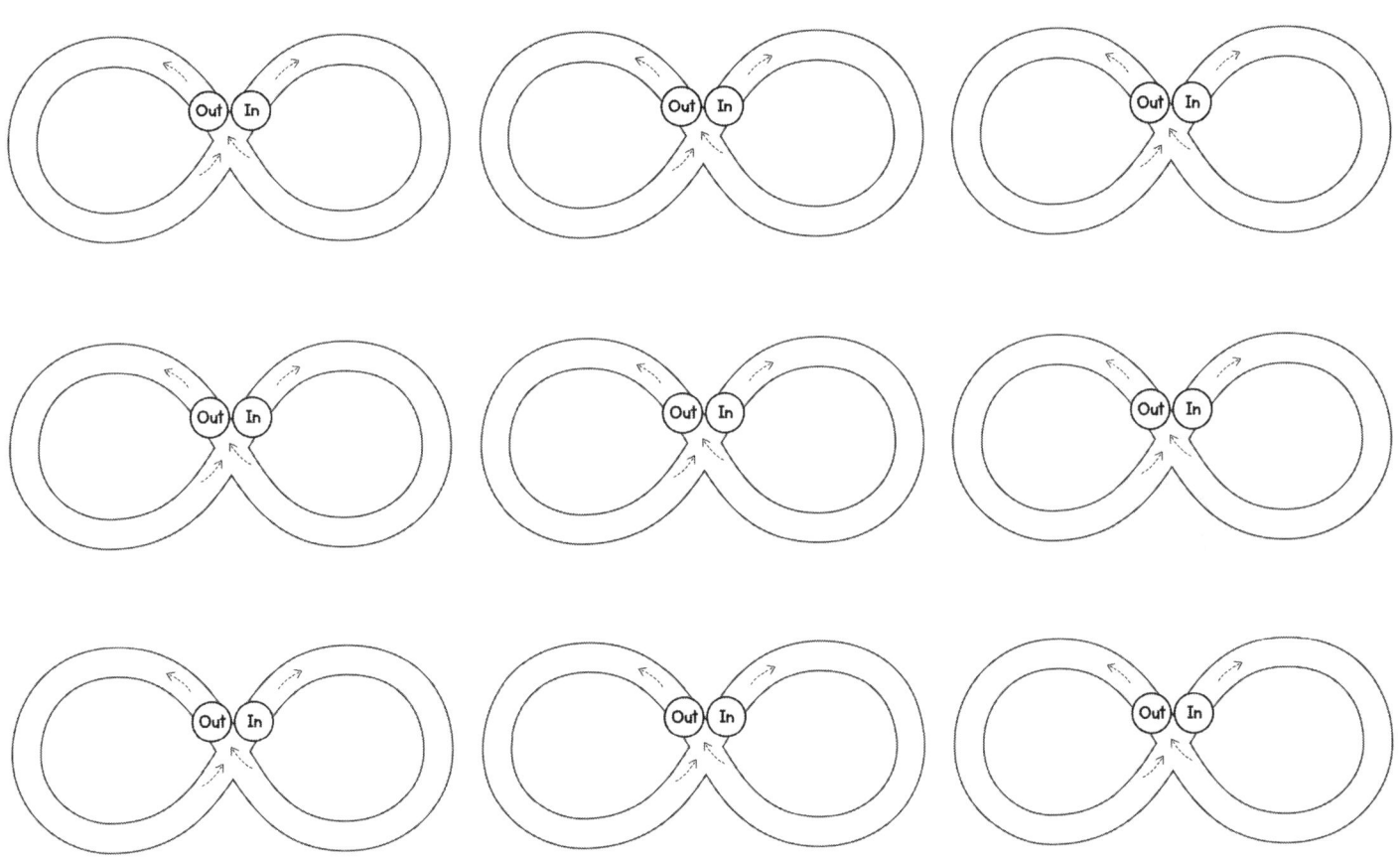

Star
Breathing

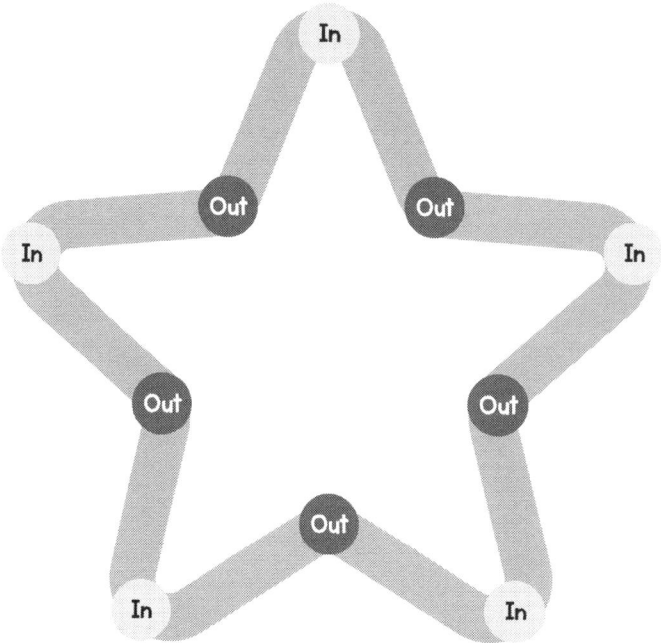

Star Breathing

Directions:

Directions:

Use your finger to trace the outline of the shape while breathing in and out as you go. Repeat this process at least 3 times or until you feel calmer.

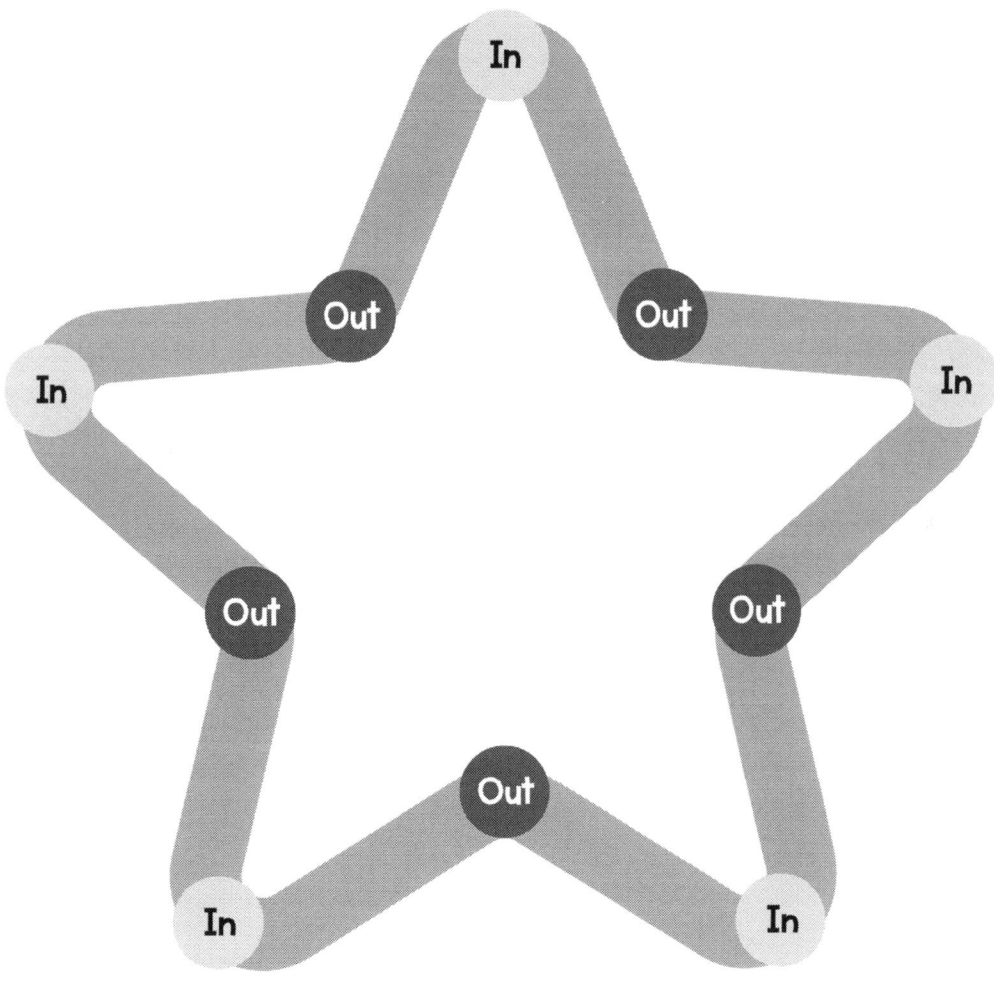

86

"Feelings are just visitors, let them come and go."

- Mooji

Star Breathing

Directions:

With any drawing tool, trace the outline of the shape while breathing in and out as you go. Repeat this process at least 3 times or until you feel calmer.

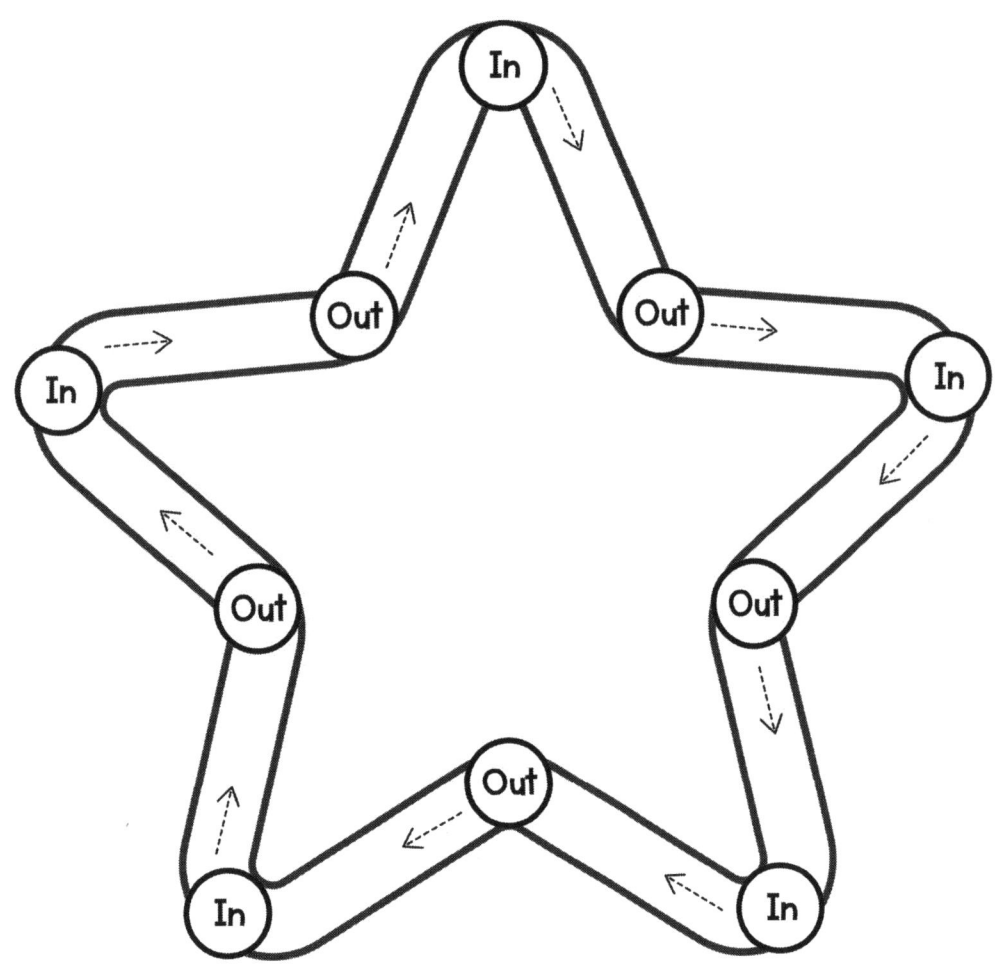

Star Breathing

Directions:

With any drawing tool, trace the outline of the shape while breathing in and out as you go. Repeat this process at least 3 times or until you feel calmer.

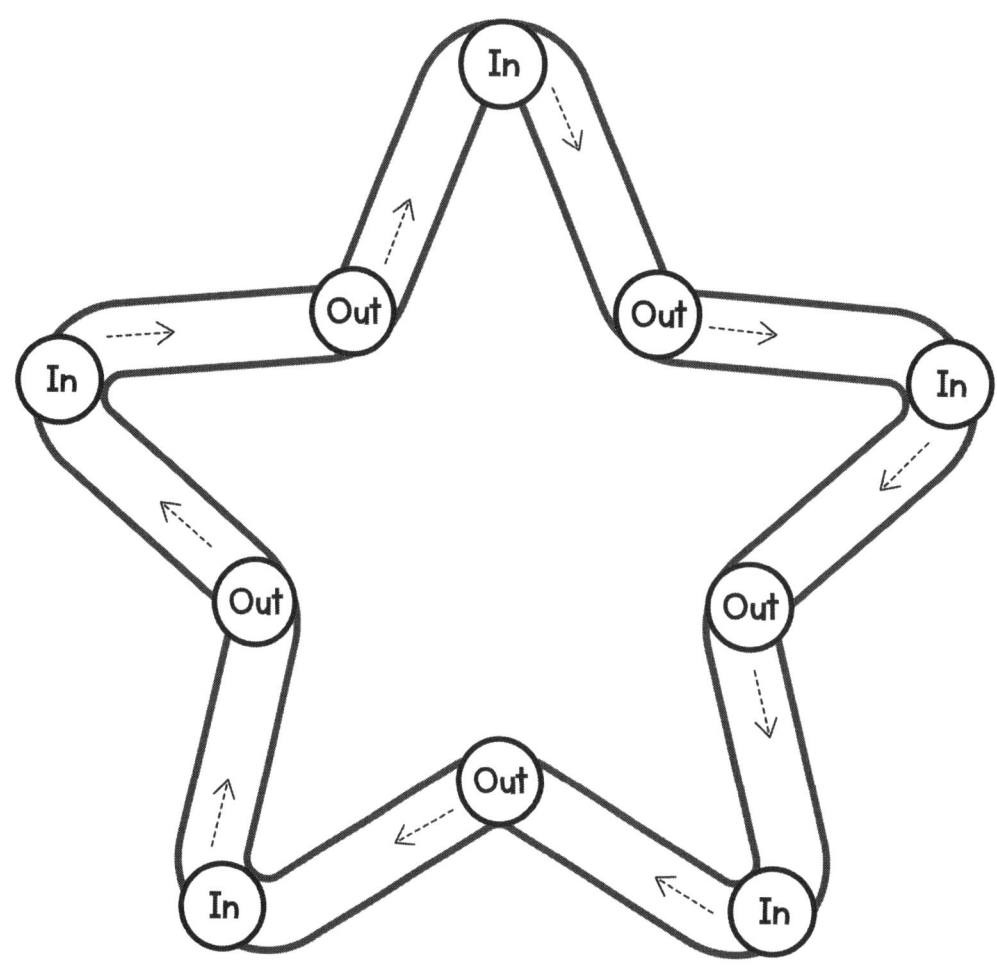

Star Breathing

With any drawing tool, trace the outline of the shape while breathing in and out as you go. Repeat this process at least 3 times or until you feel calmer.

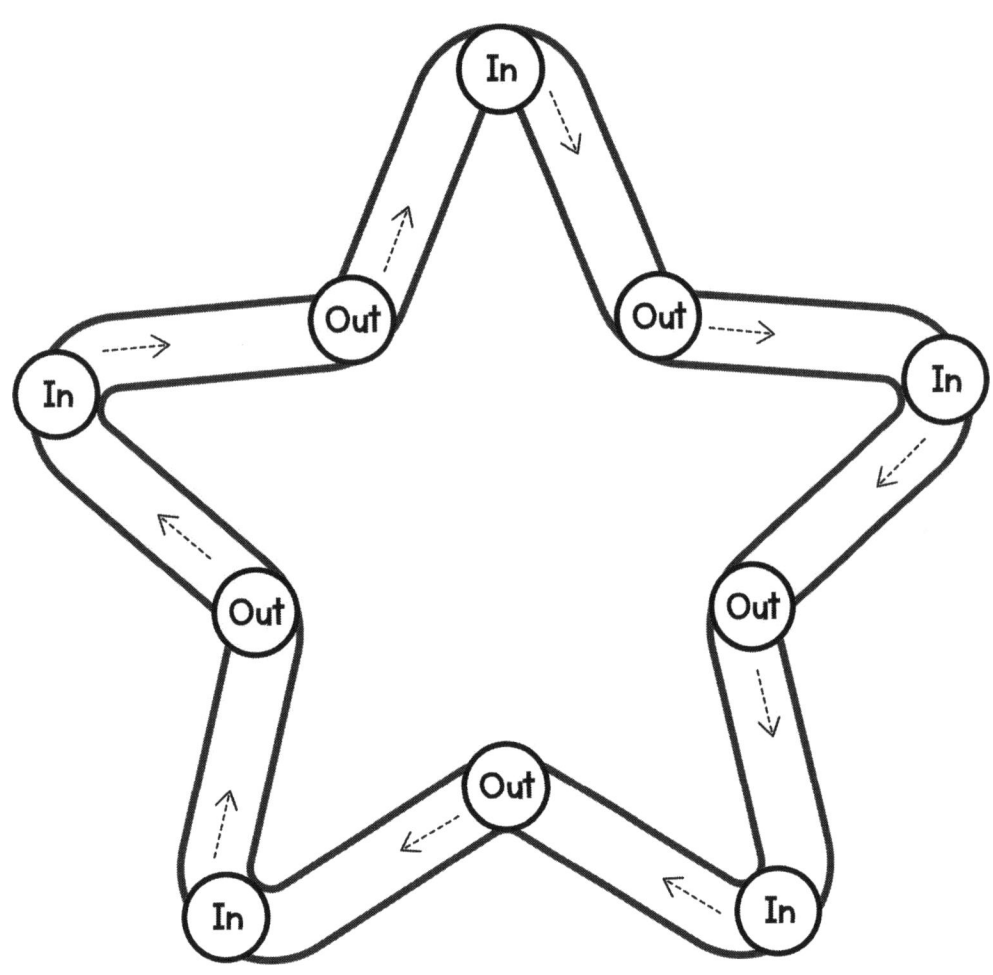

90

Star Breathing

Directions:

With any drawing tool, trace the outline of the shape while breathing in and out as you go. Repeat this process until you feel calmer.

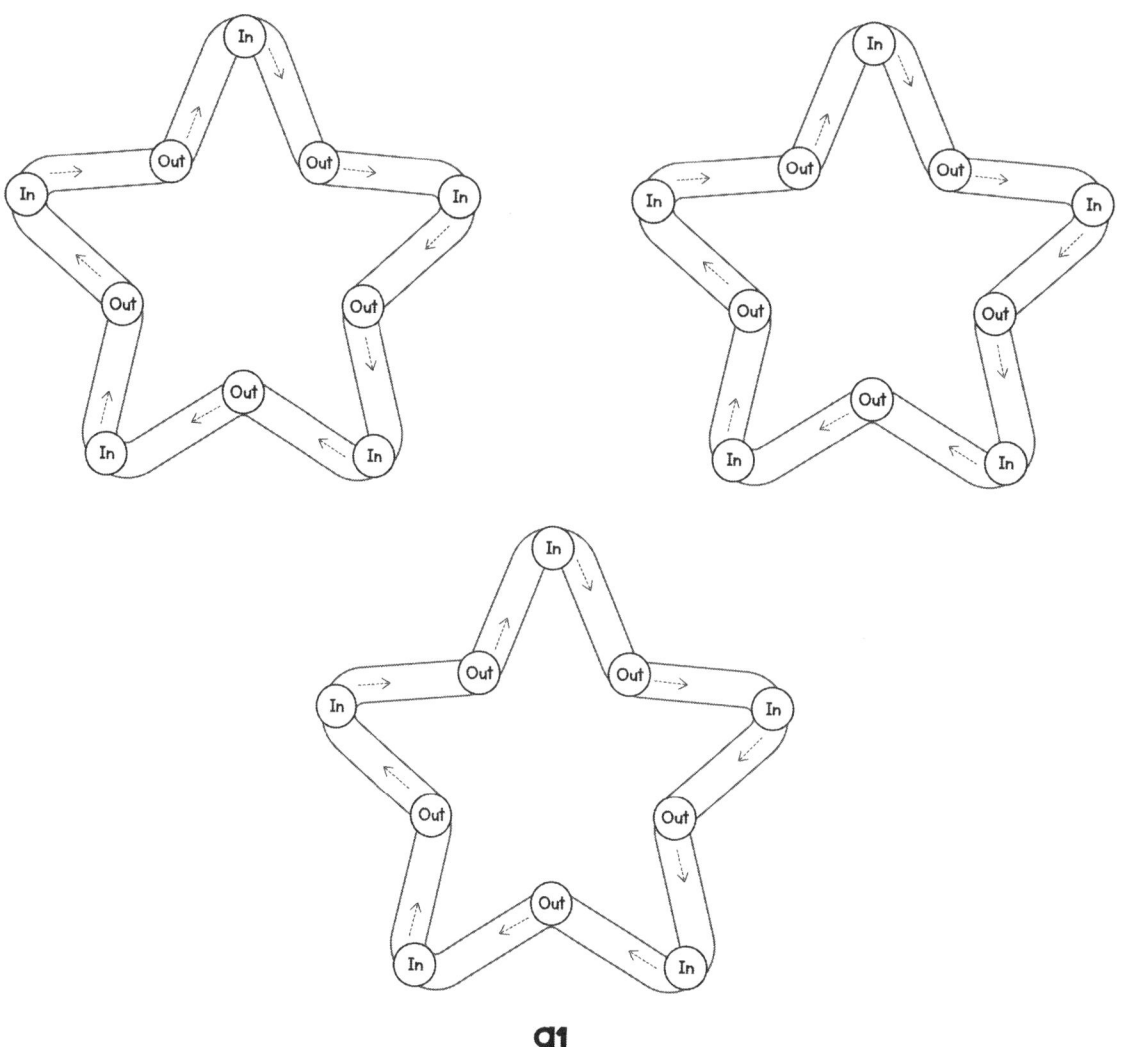

91

Star Breathing

Directions:

With any drawing tool, trace the outline of the shape while breathing in and out as you go. Repeat this process until you feel calmer.

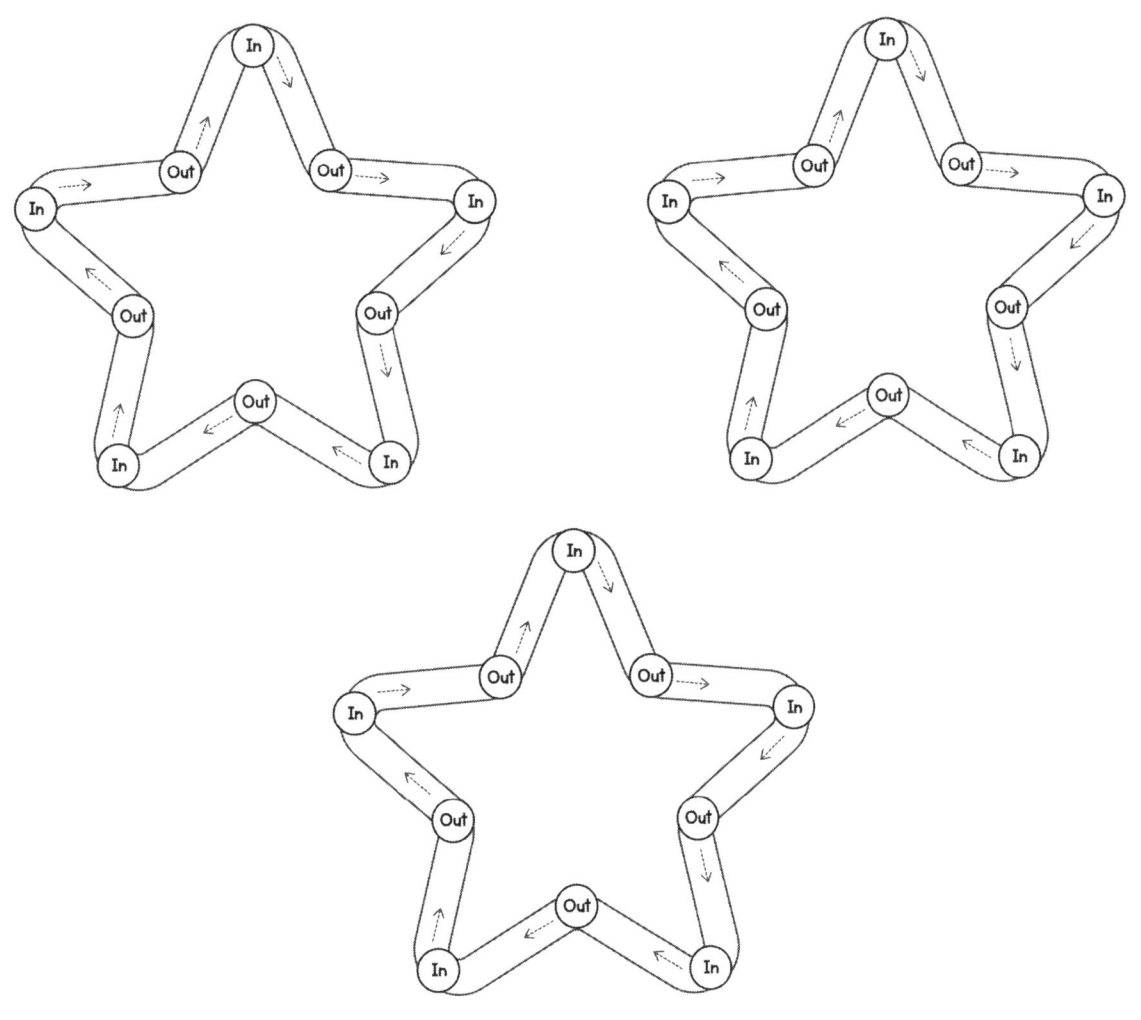

Star Breathing

Directions:

With any drawing tool, trace the outline of the shape while breathing in and out as you go. Repeat this process until you feel calmer.

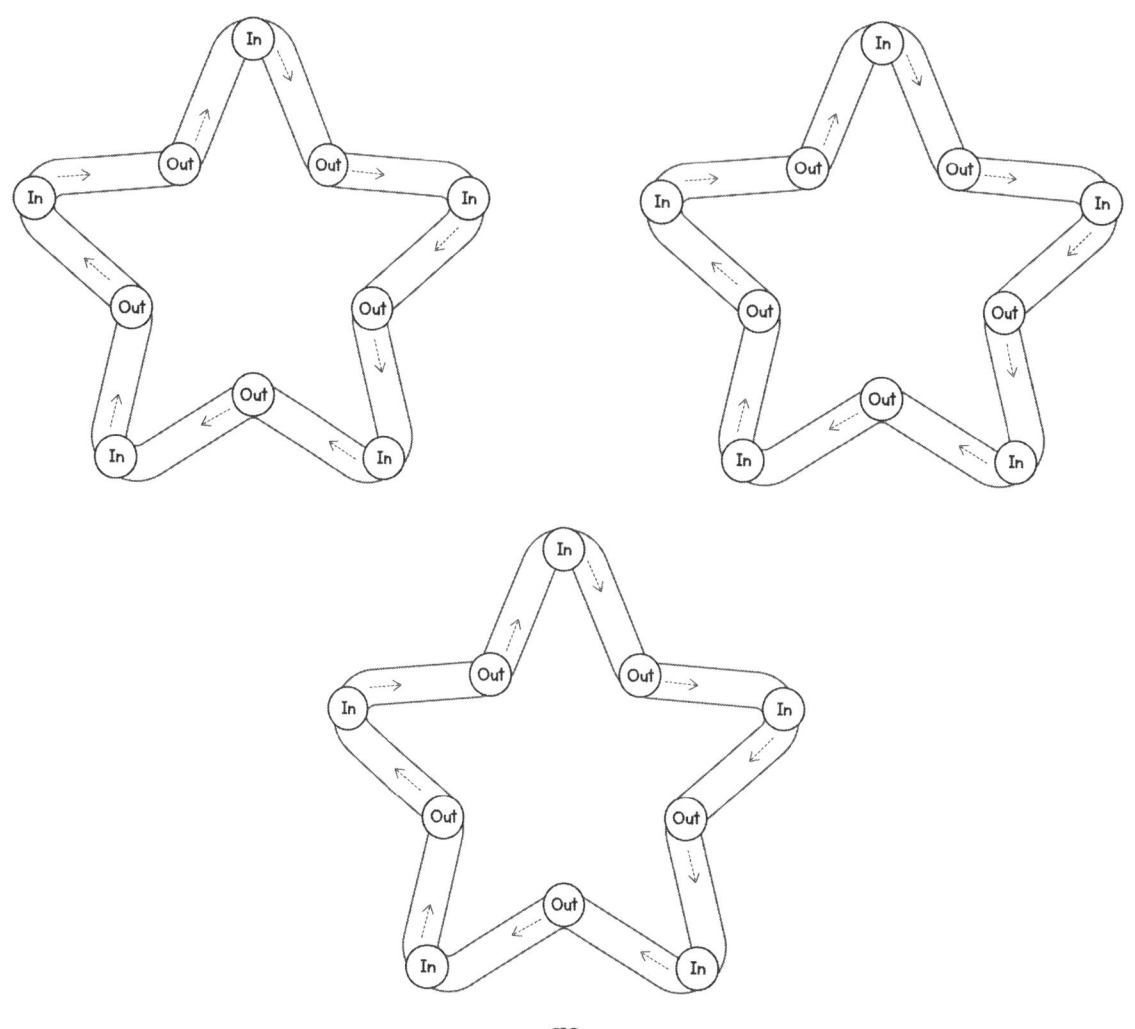

93

Star Breathing

With any drawing tool, trace the outline of the shape while breathing in and out as you go. Repeat this process until you feel calmer.

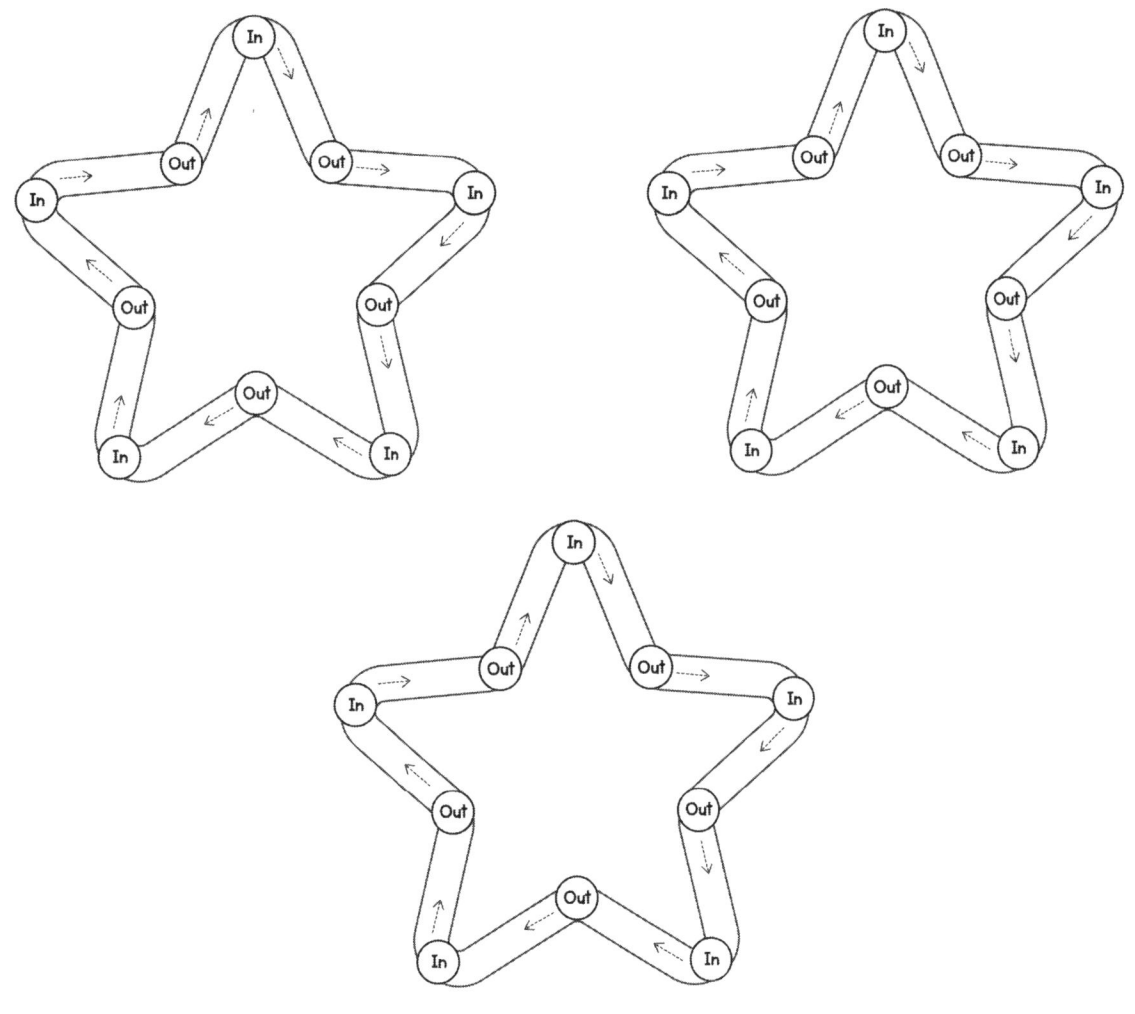

94

Star Breathing

Directions:

With any drawing tool, trace the outline of the shape while breathing in and out as you go. Repeat this process until you feel calmer.

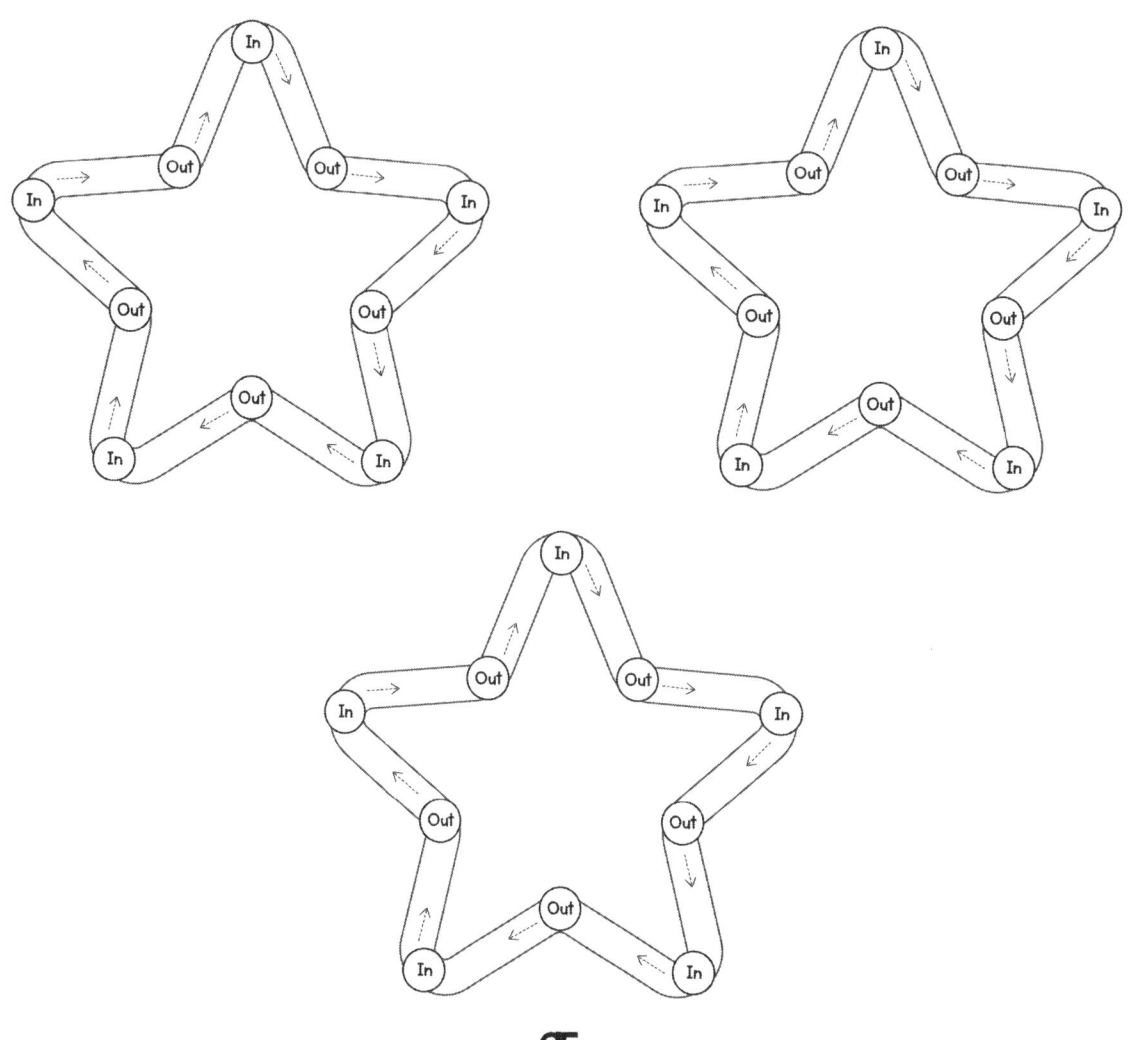

Star Breathing

Directions:

With any drawing tool, trace the outline of the shape while breathing in and out as you go. Repeat this process until you feel calmer.

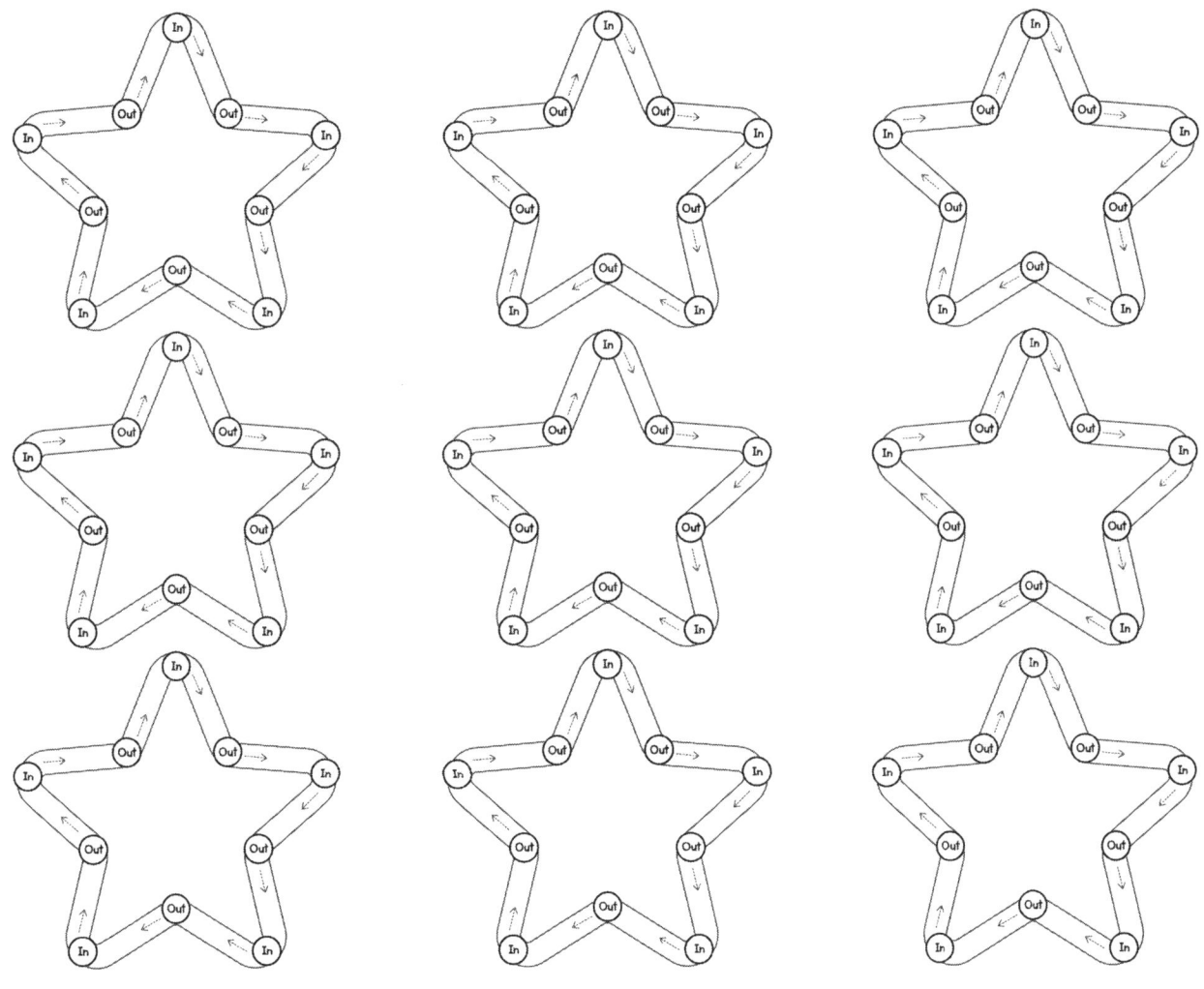

Star Breathing

Directions:

With any drawing tool, trace the outline of the shape while breathing in and out as you go. Repeat this process until you feel calmer.

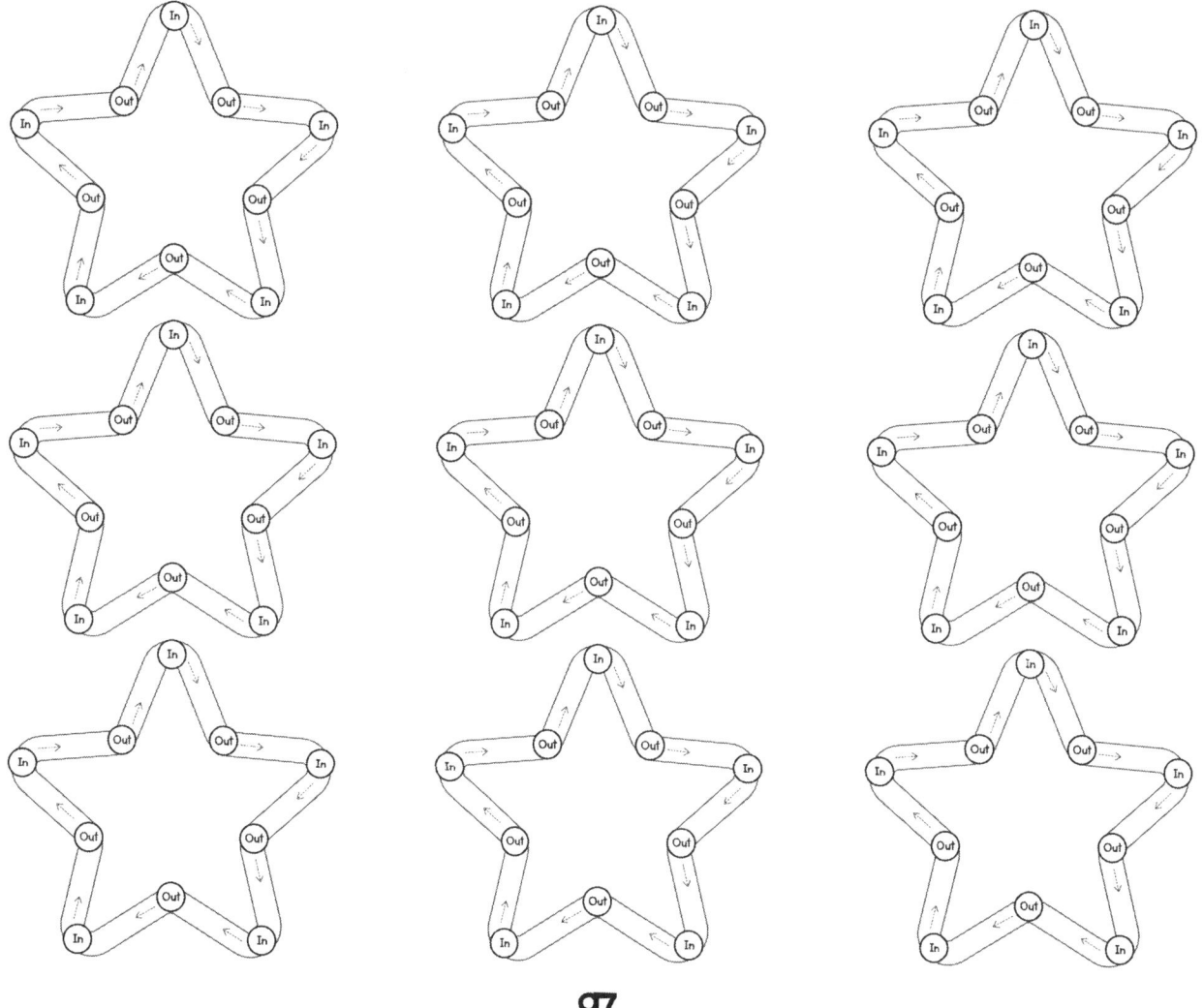

Star Breathing

Directions:

With any drawing tool, trace the outline of the shape while breathing in and out as you go. Repeat this process until you feel calmer.

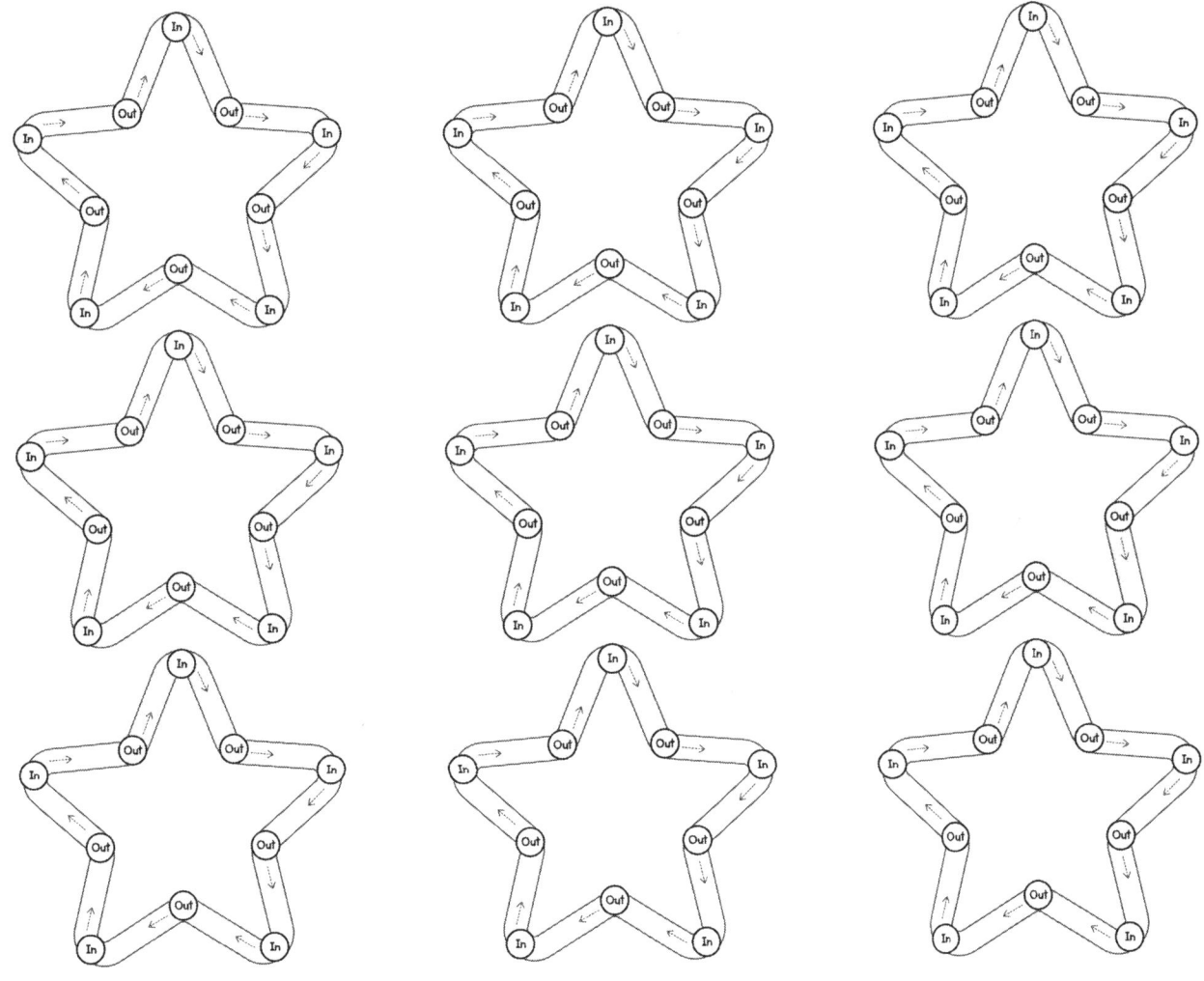

98

Star Breathing

Directions:

With any drawing tool, trace the outline of the shape while breathing in and out as you go. Repeat this process until you feel calmer.

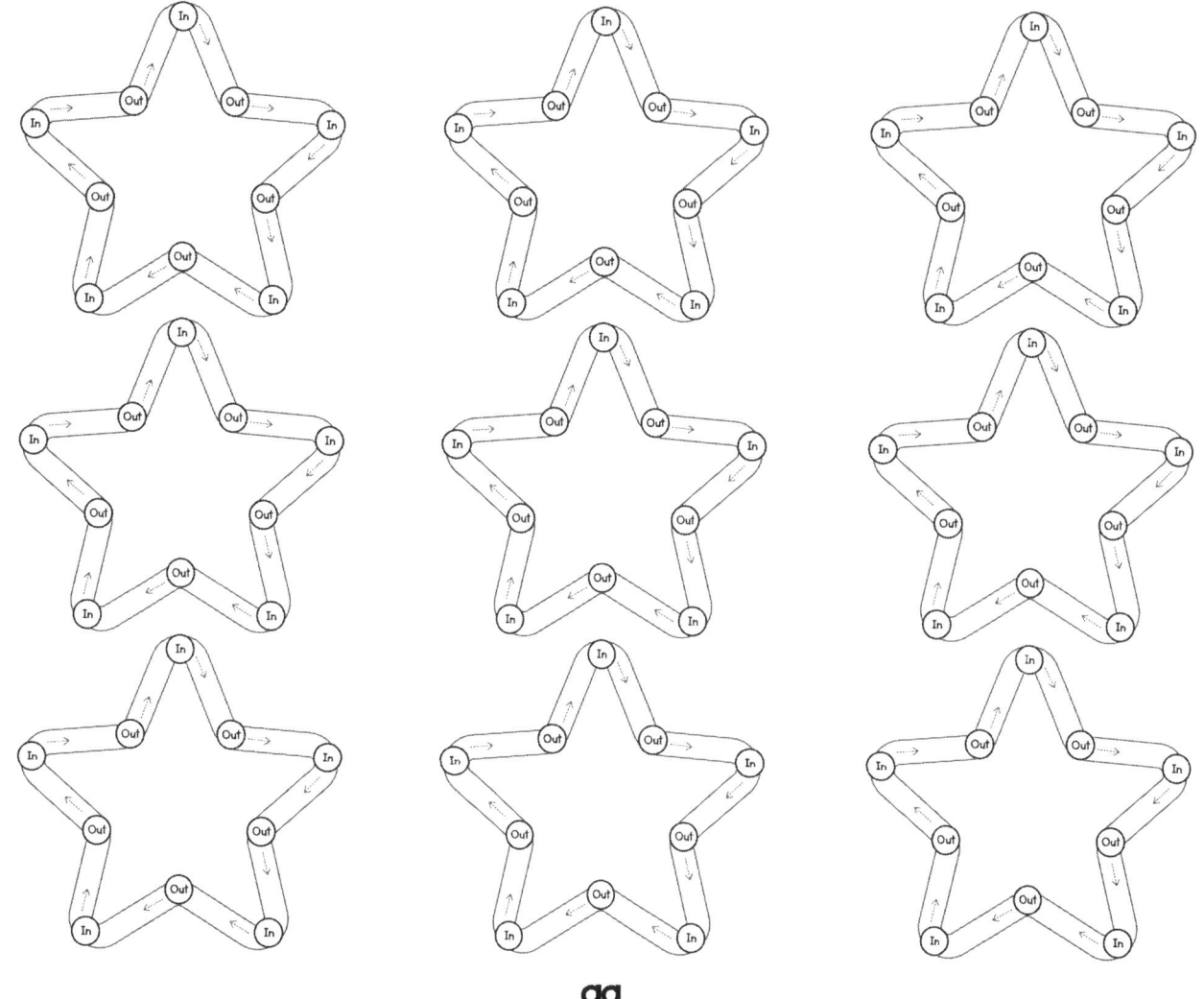

99

Star Breathing

Directions:

With any drawing tool, trace the outline of the shape while breathing in and out as you go. Repeat this process until you feel calmer.

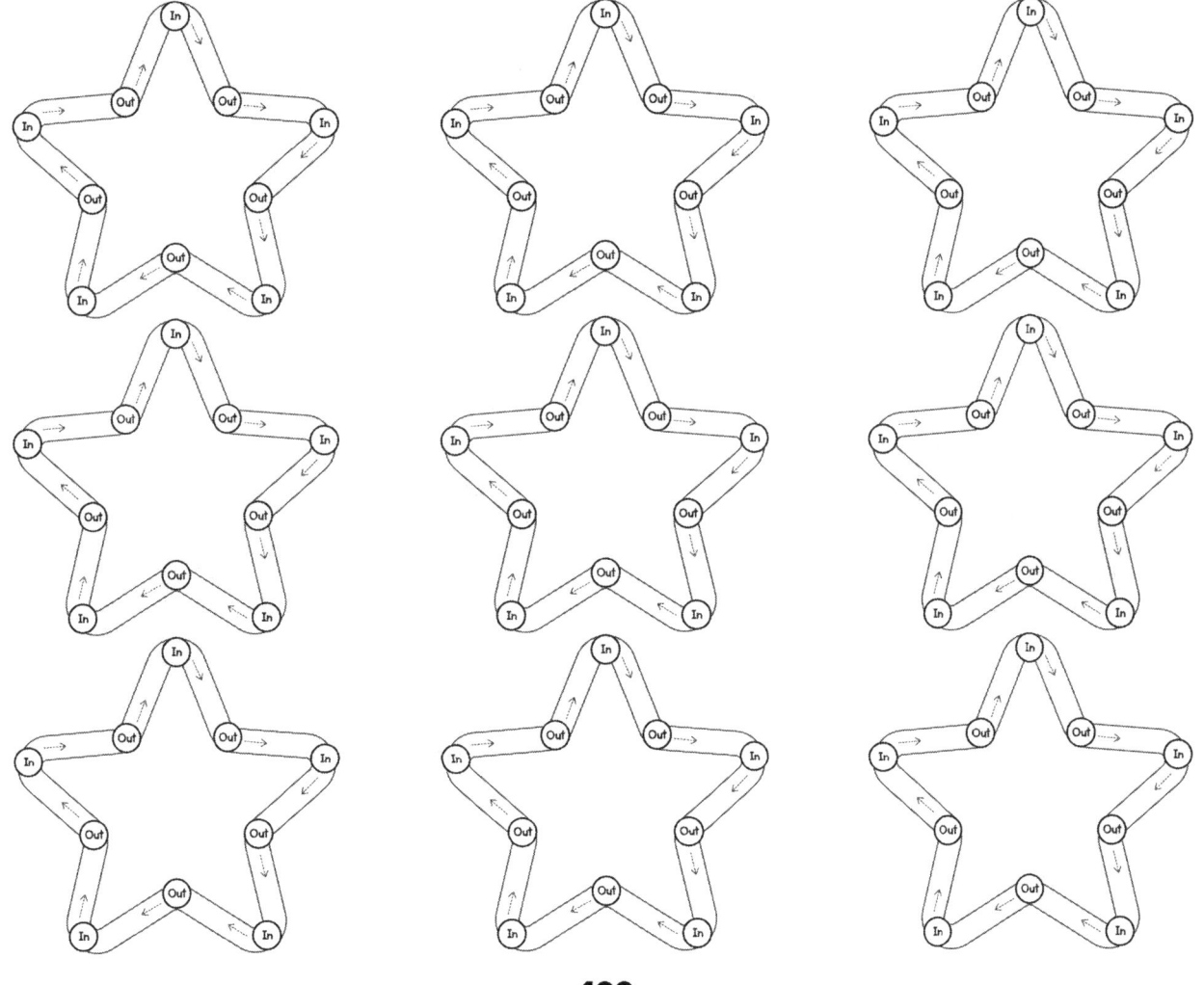

"Every breath you take is a new chance to be happy and shine bright."

- Anonymous

Check out more books from LittleYellowStar Publishing here:

Made in United States
Orlando, FL
11 July 2025

62880985R00059